The Book of Hermetic Secrets

The Emerald Tablet, The Kybalion, and their teachings

Within this fascinating book that you hold in your hands, you will discover a world beyond its printed pages. Along with its captivating story, the publisher has created a special experience for you. Beneath this text, you will find a QR code that grants you access to a carefully selected playlist on Spotify, intimately connected with the spirit of the book. Immerse yourself in the melodies and let the music transport you as you explore the plot. Additionally, you will also find another QR code that leads you to a gallery of images, capturing the essence of each moment, character, and place described in these pages. These images are available to everyone, offering you the opportunity to visualize and connect even more with the work in front of you. Enjoy this complete experience that combines literature with the senses, allowing the book to come to life in unimaginable ways.

The Book of Hermetic Secrets

The Emerald Tablet, The Kybalion, and their teachings

Illustrated and annotated edition

Translation of José Marcelo Caballero

Hermes Trismegisto & Three initiates

PAMPIA

Trismegisto, Hermes
The Book Of Hermetic Secrets : The Kybalion and their teachings / Hermes Trismegisto ; Jose Marcelo Caballero. 1a ed. Buenos Aires : Pampia, 2023.
200 p. ; 23 x 16 cm.
ISBN 9786316559043
1. Metaphysics 2. Esotericism. I. Caballero, Jose Marcelo. II. Título.
CDD 133.901

Translation of the Spanish edition: José Marcelo Caballero

Cover design and image: Maitreya Art & Design
Interior design: Maitreya Art & Design

ISBN 9786316559043
First edition: November 2023
Pampia Publishing Group
Juan Bautista Alberdi Avenue 872
C1424BYV Autonomous City of Buenos Aires
www.pampia.org

Edited in Argentina

TABLE OF CONTENTS

TABULA SMARAGDINA HERMETIS

VISITA INTERIORA TERRAE RECTIFICANDO INVENIES OCCULTUM LAPIDEM

VERBA SECRETORUM HERMETIS

"The study of Hermetic texts leads us to acknowledge the existence of a process of individuation that is expressed in archetypal symbols, which allow us to connect with our deepest and most transcendent nature".

Carl Jung

INTRODUCTION TO THE "SPIRITUAL GEMS" COLLECTION

It is a pleasure to welcome you to the "Spiritual Gems" collection, an exquisite selection of books that has been carefully curated by a great connoisseur of spirituality, César Marcelo. This collection is destined to enrich our lives in the modern world and to provide a deep understanding of the spiritual teachings that have withstood the test of time. Each book in this collection represents a significant masterpiece in the science of consciousness, chosen with utmost attention and dedication. César has dedicated countless hours to researching and selecting the most profound and enriching texts, which cover a wide range of traditions and philosophies of this nature.

The first book in the collection, a true gem, is a conjunction of the axioms from two emblematic works: The Emerald Tablet and The Kybalion. This book merges the knowledge from these two important works to offer a comprehensive and enriching view of the human spirit. The maxims contained within these pages have been transmitted through the centuries and contain a timeless wisdom that has the power to transform our lives.

It is important to highlight that each book in this collection has been crafted with great care and attention. Each word has been precisely selected, and the teachings are presented in a clear and accessible manner, so that everyone can benefit from them, regardless of their level of spiritual experience. The curator of this collection is a recognized expert in spirituality and has dedicated his life to the study and practice of various spiritual traditions. His profound knowledge and passion for these subjects are reflected in each book selected for "Spiritual Gems". His aim is to provide a transformative experience through these works, allowing us to delve into our own spiritual growth and expand our understanding of the world around us.

We invite you to immerse yourself in this unique collection, to discover the richness of its contents, and to allow these beautiful books to inspire and guide your lives. "Spiritual Gems" is much more than just a collection of books; it is a treasure for the soul, an invitation to explore the mysteries of our existence and to discover our deepest connection with the universe. Join us on this journey towards enlightenment and let these written words illuminate your path.

EXPLORING THE HERMETIC MYSTERIES

The quest for knowledge and understanding of reality has captivated humanity throughout the centuries. In this journey in search of truth, numerous traditions and philosophies have emerged, offering unique perspectives and tools to unravel the secrets of the universe. Among these traditions are alchemy and Hermeticism, which have left a profound mark on the history of human wisdom.

Within the vast corpus of alchemy and Hermeticism, two texts in particular have captured the imagination of knowledge seekers and have influenced the development of philosophical and esoteric thought: *The Emerald Tablet and The Kybalion*. Although these texts are independent in their origin and presentation, they share a common thread that unites them in the exploration of Hermetic mysteries.

The Emerald Tablet, also known as the *Tabula Smaragdina*, is a brief alchemical text attributed to *Hermes Trismegistus*, a legendary figure in the alchemical tradition. The Tablet has remained shrouded in mystery and has been the subject of countless interpretations over the centuries. According to legend, it was found in a tomb in Egypt and contains the fundamental principles of alchemy. Its fourteen enigmatic poetic sentences have fascinated alchemists, philosophers, and esotericists, and have served as a starting point for understanding alchemical processes and the nature of the universe.

On the other hand, *The Kybalion*, a work that compiles and explains Hermetic principles, has left a significant mark in the modern esoteric and philosophical sphere. Although it does not make explicit reference to the Emerald Tablet, The Kybalion is inspired by Hermetic principles and offers guidance for understanding reality and achieving personal transformation. The seven fundamental principles of The Kybalion, which include the principles of mentalism, correspondence, vibration, polarity, rhythm, cause and effects, and generation, are considered essential pillars for understanding the nature of the universe and our role within it.

Both texts explore the relationship between the microcosm and macrocosm, emphasizing the interconnection and unity in all things. The Emerald Tablet states that "as above, so below; as below, so above", while The Kybalion, in its second axiom, discusses the correspondence between the mental, emotional, and material planes. Both texts invite us to reflect on the nature of reality and our capacity to understand and transform it.

In this book, we will embark on an exciting journey of exploration into the Hermetic mysteries, merging the wisdom of the Emerald Tablet and The Kybalion. Our intention is to delve into the depths of these texts, unravel their teachings, and discover how they intertwine to provide a more complete understanding of reality and human potential. We will start with the Emerald Tablet, examining each of its fourteen sentences with a critical eye and an open mind. We will explore its symbolism and hidden meaning, challenging the limits of our understanding and embracing the richness of its alchemical poetry. As we uncover layers of knowledge and possible interpretations, we will delve into the fascinating world of transmutation, the unity of opposites, and the quest for the philosopher's stone.

After establishing a solid foundation in *the Emerald Tablet,* we will venture into the vast territory of the Hermetic principles presented in The Kybalion. We will explore each of the seven principles, dissecting their meaning and unraveling their applicability in our daily lives. From the principle of mentalism, which invites us to recognize the power of our thoughts, to the principle of cause and effect, which urges us to take responsibility for our actions, we will immerse ourselves in the practical knowledge they offer.

As we progress in our journey, we will seek the connections and synergies between both texts; we will examine how they complement and enrich each other, how they intertwine in their exploration of the nature of reality and personal transformation. Through examples and reflections, we will discover how understanding the Hermetic principles can deepen our interpretation of the Emerald Tablet, and how the symbolism of the latter can expand our understanding of the Hermetic principles. Furthermore, this book will not be limited to theory and intellectual analysis, but will also explore the practical applications of these principles in our daily life. Through exercises, meditations, and reflections, we will invite the reader to experience and apply them in their own path of personal and spiritual growth. From cultivating mindfulness to transforming our relationships and awakening our inner potential, we will discover how these ancient teachings can illuminate and enrich our path towards self realization.

Prepare to delve into a fascinating territory, where alchemy intertwines with philosophy, where the symbolic meets the practical, and where the quest for truth becomes a personal and transformative experience. As we delve deeper into the secrets of the Emerald Tablet and unravel the Hermetic principles of The Kybalion, we will immerse ourselves in an ocean of ancient wisdom that has withstood the test of time.

It's important to note that this work does not aim to provide definitive answers or absolute truths. These are texts that have been subject to interpretation and debate over the centuries, and each individual can find their own understanding and meaning in them. Our purpose is to present an enriching exploration of these teachings, providing tools and perspectives that can inspire and guide readers on their own journey of discovery.

THE EMERALD TABLET

"The Emerald Tablet is a notable example of Hermetic and alchemical wisdom. It represents the quest for unity and the transformation of the individual. Its symbols and teachings have had a profound impact on analytical psychology and the process of individuation".

Carl Jung

HERMETIS TRISMEGISTI

PHOENICUM ÆGYPTIORUM
Sed et aliarum Gentium
MONARCHÆ CONDITORIS

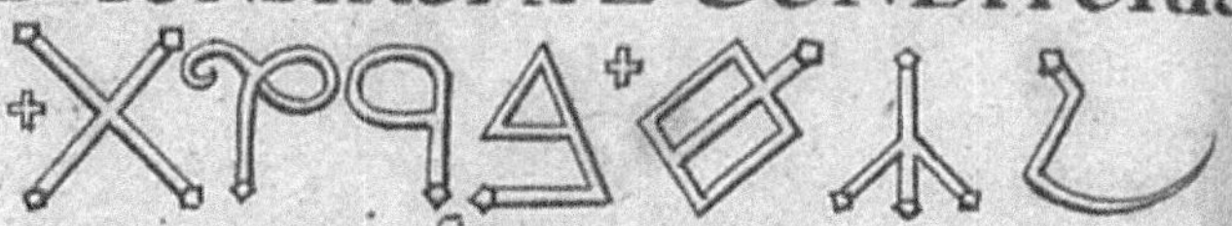

ſive

TABULA SMARAGDINA

à ſitu temerariȷſq;
nunc demum priſtino Genio
Vindicata per
WILHELMUM CHRISTOPHORUM
KRIEGSMANNUM.

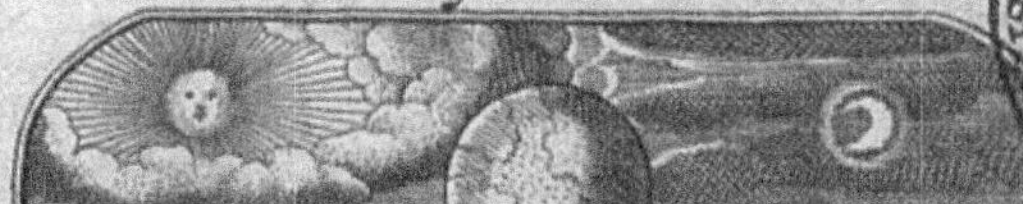

DEUTER: XXXIII. vers: 13.14.16.
Benedictum eſt à DOMINO terræ ejus pretioſo
Coeli fructu, Rore; et ex abyſso cubante infer-
nè: pretioſo fructu proventuum Solis; et
pretioſo fructu influentiæ Lunæ: pretioſo deniq; fructu terræ, uberta-
teq; ejus.
Adjectum eſt
Teſtamentum Arnoldi de Villa Nova

The Emerald Tablet emerges as a resplendent jewel in the vast treasure of Hermetic and alchemical tradition, a path of ancient wisdom intertwined with the mists of ancient Egypt and Greece. At the heart of this legend stands Hermes Trismegistus, an enigmatic figure rising as a mystical amalgamation of Egyptian and Greek deities. Endowed with supreme wisdom and a gift for conveying esoteric knowledge, Hermes becomes the guardian of the tablet, a legendary inheritance that resonates with echoes from ancient times. Although its physical authenticity is lost in the mists of the past, it has left its mark on history in various forms and versions. It is believed that in its original form, this sacred script rested on an emerald slab, flashing with its luminous green the hidden mystery in its engraved words. However, it is important to highlight that these descriptions delve into the legend and the alchemical tradition surrounding it, as in reality, the text has been preserved in ancient manuscripts, silent witnesses of its ethereal essence. The enduring narrative tells that it emerged from the shadows in the ancestral lands of Egypt, evoking the image of a treasure buried for eons. This archeological enigma, with its aura of mystery and ancient history, has transcended through time and has been cautiously transmitted among alchemical and esoteric circles, whispering forgotten secrets and awakening an unquenchable longing in those who yearn to unveil its mysteries. This discovery sparks the imagination and evokes images of intrepid explorers venturing into the depths of ancient crypts in search of hidden answers. Was it found among the funeral treasures of a forgotten pharaoh? Or perhaps it rests in a subterranean chamber protected by hieroglyphs and deadly traps? The answer is lost in the whispers of time, leaving room for imagination and wonder.

These precious relics, on papyrus, parchment, or paper, carry in their letters the vibrant heritage of the Tablet, immortalizing its message through the centuries. Written in various languages such as Latin and Arabic, these later copies of the original text have been the subject of meticulous study and careful translation, in a tireless effort to expose the teachings imbued in their lines. Thus, while the Emerald Tablet remains shrouded in a veil of enigma, its essence transcends the barriers of time and space, captivating those who seek to decipher the deepest secrets of the universe and the human being. As a luminous beacon in the vastness of Hermetic wisdom, it continues to resonate in the hearts and minds of truth seekers, inviting them to explore the wonders of alchemy and to embark on a journey of inner transformation.

"Emerald, the precious stone that lends its name to this sacred tablet, becomes a symbol of purity and clarity. Its green radiance evokes the freshness of spring meadows and the vitality emanating from nature itself. Although it is not a physical emerald slab that contains the message, its symbolic presence invokes an ethereal beauty and a connection with the mysteries of life and alchemical knowledge. Carefully traced letters stand as silent witnesses to the transcendence of Hermetic wisdom. The ancient and resonant language becomes the canvas that embraces the elegantly imprinted words, whispering to the reader's ear the ancient wisdom hidden within its yellowed pages".

> The Emerald Tablet of Hermes Trismegistus, the Egyptian Thoth, is the cornerstone of alchemy. Philosophers quote it incessantly, which is why it is important to be familiar with this document.
>
> It can be found in all the significant collections of Hermetic treaties: *Theatrum Chemicum, Bibliotheca Chemica Curiosa, and Bibliotheca Chemica Contracta of Albinus,* among others.

Although each copy is but a shadow of the original, the manuscripts encompass the very essence of the original tablet. Their pages, filled with mystery and promise, awaken the curiosity and longing of those who seek to unravel their hidden secrets. Through scholarship and patience, students of alchemy have delved into every line and every word, searching for the key that will unlock the doors of knowledge and reveal the path of inner transformation. In each stroke and every symbol of the manuscript, a profound worldview and an intricate connection between the microcosm and the macrocosm are revealed. Metaphors and enigmas are masterfully interwoven, inviting the reader to embark on a journey of self discovery and exploration of the universe's secrets. The Emerald Tablet becomes a beacon of light in the midst of darkness, guiding those who are willing to challenge the limits of their understanding and embark on a path of wisdom and revelation.

> Frances Yates: "The Emerald Tablet has been the subject of interpretations and analysis throughout the centuries. It is an enigmatic text that has captured the imagination of numerous scholars and alchemists. Its importance lies in its vision of nature and hidden knowledge".

1. "Verum, sine mendacio, certum et verissimum"	"True, without lie, certain, and very true.
2. "Quod est inferius est sicut quod est superius, et quod est superius est sicut quod est inferius, ad perpetranda miracula rei unius" –	As above, so below; as below, so above, to perform the miracles of the one thing.
3. "Et sicut res omnes fuerunt ab uno, meditatione unius, sic omnes res natae fuerunt ab hac una re, adaptatione"	And as all things have arisen from one by the contemplation of one, so all things are born from this one thing by adaptation.
4. "Pater eius est Sol, mater eius est Luna, portavit illud Ventus in ventre suo, nutrix eius terra est"	Its father is the Sun, its mother the Moon; the wind has carried it in its belly, the Earth is its nurse.
5. Pater omnis telesmi totius mundi est hic"	The father of all perfection in the whole world is here.
6. Virtus eius integra est si versa fuerit in terram	Its power is complete if it is turned to Earth.
7. Separabis terram ab igne, subtile ab spisso, suaviter, magno cum ingenio	You will separate the Earth from the Fire, the subtle from the dense, gently, with great skill.
8. Ascendit a terra in coelum, iterumque descendit in terram, et recipit vim superiorum et inferiorum	It ascends from Earth to Heaven and descends again to Earth, and receives the power of the higher and of the lower.
9. Sic habebis gloriam totius mundi	Thus, you will have the glory of the whole world.
10. Ideo fugiet a te omnis obscuritas	Therefore, all obscurity will flee from you.
11. Haec est totius fortitudinis fortitudo fortis, quia vincet omnem rem subtilem, omnemque solidam penetrabit	This is the strength of all strengths, for it will overcome every subtle thing and penetrate every solid thing.
12. Sic mundus creatus est	So the world was created.
13. Hinc erunt adaptationes mirabiles, quarum modus est hic	From this will come amazing adaptations, of which the means is here.
14. Itaque vocatus sum Hermes Trismegistus, habens tres partes philosophiae totius mundi	That is why I am called Hermes Trismegistus, having the three parts of the philosophy of the whole world.

HISTORY WHISPERS TO US

"The Emerald Tablet is a mysterious and enigmatic text that I have studied with great interest. It contains universal principles that can be applied to various fields of knowledge, including science and philosophy".

Isaac Newton

In the fourteen enigmatic sentences, we can find a jewel of Wisdom, a compendium of Truth that transcends the limitations of time and space.

1. "Verum, sine mendacio, certum et verissimum"

"True, without lie, certain, and very true".

The first premise of the Tablet reveals the infallible nature of Truth. Master Hermes Trismegistus, with his wise and experienced voice, assures that the teachings presented in these lines are truthful, free from deceit and fallacies. In them, there is no room for ambiguity or confusion, even if it sounds abstruse or dark to those who have not uncovered the deepest secrets. Truth, in its essence, always remains in the shadows, veiled from profane eyes, until an enlightened mind brings its light to reveal it in all its magnificence.

This proposition urges us to seek truth in all areas of our life. It reminds us of the importance of honesty and sincerity in our actions and words. In our daily life, we can apply this premise by being aware of our intentions and ensuring that our actions are aligned with truth and authenticity. This involves acting with integrity, being honest with ourselves and others, and seeking truth in our interactions and decisions.

2. "Quod est inferius est sicut quod est superius, et quod est superius est sicut quod est inferius, ad perpetranda miracula rei unius"

"As above, so below; as below, so above, to perform the miracles of the one thing".

The second sentence transports us to the intimate link between the microcosm and macrocosm. Hermes reveals to us the divine reflection present at every level of existence. What happens in the heavens, in the celestial spheres, finds its correspondence on Earth, in every atom, in every human being. The cosmos and its mysterious designs have a direct influence on the planets and, consequently, on our own earthly existence. We are living witnesses of the cosmic dance that governs our lives, a reminder of our unbreakable connection with the universe.

This speaks to the interconnection between all levels of existence. It shows us that everything that happens at the microcosmic level has a correspondence in the macrocosm, and vice versa. In our daily life, this invites us to recognize that our individual actions and decisions have an impact on the broader world. It reminds us that our personal choices and our way of living can have a significant effect on our own lives and on the environment around us. It encourages us to be aware of our connections with the world and to recognize that our actions can influence the harmony and balance of the whole.

3. "Et sicut res omnes fuerunt ab uno, meditatione unius, sic omnes res natae fuerunt ab hac una re, adaptatione"

"And just as all things arose from one, by the meditation of one, so all things were born from this one thing by adaptation".

The third proposition leads us to the miracle of unity. Although we may feel separated and isolated, this is an illusion that we must transcend. Each particle, no matter how minute, contains the very essence of the Whole. In every atom beats the pulse of the universe. We are an indivisible part of creation, united in all our facets to the vast cosmic fabric. The awakening of this understanding is a true miracle, a revelation that allows us to appreciate the wonder and interconnectedness of all existence

> "The Emerald Tablet is a fascinating text that combines Hermetic philosophy with alchemy. Its teachings on transmutation and the search for inner knowledge resonate with the spiritual quest and the expansion of consciousness."
>
> Terence McKenna

This condition speaks to us of the fundamental unity of all things and how they arise from a common source. It invites us to recognize that everything in the universe is interconnected and that our individual actions can have an impact on the broader fabric of existence. In our daily lives, this encourages us to practice reflection and meditation, to connect with our own essence, and to be aware of how our actions and choices can influence the world around us. It urges us to adapt to circumstances and to seek harmony in our interactions with others and with nature.

4. "Pater eius est Sol, mater eius est Luna, portavit illud Ventus in ventre suo, nutrix eius terra est"

"His father is the Sun, his mother the Moon, the wind carried it in its belly, the Earth is its nurse".

The fourth sentence immerses us in the law of evolution and adaptation. Everything has arisen from the One, from the Eternal Father, and has been shaped and transformed over time and forms. The universe, in its entirety, proceeds from the absolute power of the Divine. Every manifestation, every form, every creature finds its origin in constant adaptation and evolution. And the day will come when all things will return to their origin, in a cosmic embrace that unites everything created and uncreated in a single divine breath.

This premise uses metaphors to describe the influences and fundamental elements that con-tribute to the formation and development of all things. It reminds us of the importance of recognizing and honoring the natural forces that surround us. In our daily lives, this invites us to have a deep respect and connection with nature, to recognize our interdependence with the natural world, and to care for the environment in which we live. It also reminds us that we are part of something larger and that our roots are deeply intertwined with the universe.

5. "Pater omnis telesmi totius mundi est hic"

"The father of all perfection in the whole world is here".

The fifth proposition speaks to us through the magical symbols of the four elements of nature. The Sun, as blazing fire, the Moon, as serene water reflecting its silvery light, the wind carrying its secrets in its invisible currents, and the Earth, our nurturing mother sustaining all life. These elements are the foundation of our existence, the pillars that uphold the universe in its eternal dance. In their conjunction and harmony, the spiritual power of the human being to perceive and rise beyond their own nature is revealed, to manipulate and understand the subtle forces that surround us. In the symbol of the five pointed star, with its apex pointing upwards, we find man in his effort to master and balance these elements, being aware of his role as a co-creator in the vast cosmic tapestry.

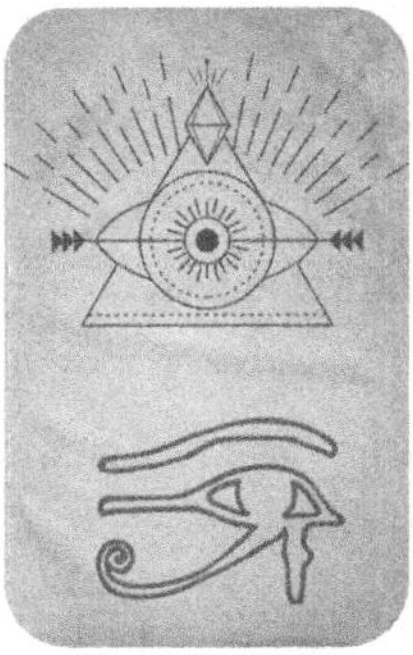

This premise speaks to us of the human potential to achieve perfection and spiritual evolution. It reminds us that within us lies the capacity for growth and development in all aspects of our life. In our daily life, this inspires us to seek perfection in our actions, thoughts, and emotions. It urges us to cultivate virtues such as compassion, wisdom, and kindness, and to work on our personal and spiritual growth.

6. "Virtus eius integra est si versa fuerit in terram"

"Its power is complete if it is transformed to Earth".

The sixth sentence immerses us in the very presence of the Creator, the source of all existence. The father of all the telesm of the world is here, present in every corner and every moment. His strength and power unfold in every manifestation of life, in every atom, and in every thought. In our exploration and understanding of the mysteries of alchemy, we find the divine spark that drives us to create and transform, to turn the ordinary into extraordinary. The ability to make gold, in its broadest sense, is within our reach, as we are carriers of the creative potential of the universe.

This premise speaks to us about the importance of manifesting and putting into practice our potential and virtues in the physical world. It reminds us that true power and fulfillment are found in action and the materialization of our capabilities. In our daily lives, this motivates us to translate our ideas and skills into concrete actions. It invites us to use our gifts and talents to contribute to our own well-being and that of others, and to make the world a better place.

TABULA SMARAGDINA HERMETIS.

VISITA
INTERIORA
TERRÆ
RECTIFICANDO
INVENIES
OCCULTUM
LAPIDEM

VERBA SECRETORUM HERMETIS.

7. "Separabis terram ab igne, subtile ab spisso, suaviter, magno cum ingenio"

"You will separate the Earth from the Fire, the subtle from the dense, gently, with great skill".

And thus, in the seventh sentence, the importance of recognizing the value and intrinsic purpose of each thing is revealed to us. Everything has a positive and negative side, a surface where the best of its essence shines. It is the task of the human being, endowed with superior art and wisdom, to discern and take the best from each element, from each experience, to create something superior. Just as Mother Earth nurtures and cares for all forms of life, we, as conscious beings, are called to honor and elevate everything around us, creating a sacred communion with Creation itself.

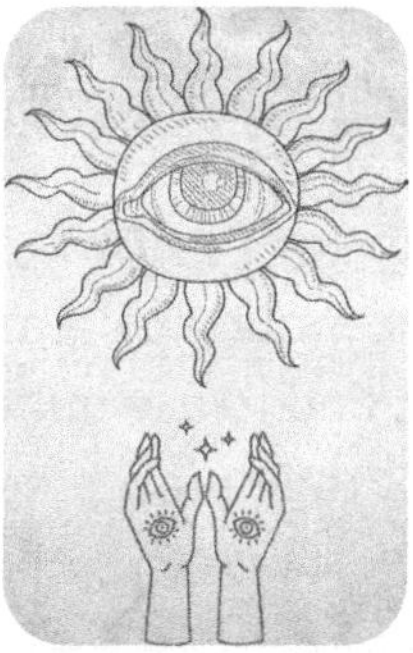

This premise speaks to us about the need to discern and separate the essential from the superfluous in our lives. It urges us to be skilled in identifying and valuing what truly matters, and to detach ourselves from what limits or distracts us. In our daily lives, this involves cultivating mental clarity and wisdom to make informed decisions. It encourages us to be aware of our priorities and to focus on what nourishes us and drives us towards our growth and well-being.

8. "Ascendit a terra in coelum, iterumque descendit in terram, et recipit vim superiorum et inferiorum"

"It ascends from the Earth to the Heaven, and descends again to the Earth, and receives the power of the higher and the lower".

In the eighth sentence, the ability to separate the dense from the subtle is revealed to us. The Earth, representing materiality, and Fire, representing spiritual energy, are presented as opposite poles that need to be discerned with delicacy and wisdom. The capacity to differentiate and understand the more subtle aspects of existence, transcending superficial appearances, is a gift reserved for those who cultivate meditation and reflection. Through this discernment, we are capable of recognizing the intrinsic value of all things and separating what is beneficial from what is not. Just as the alchemist can extract the perfume of a rose without needing the flower itself, we can learn to extract the essence of each experience and use them for our own evolution. This teaching also invites us to recognize our dual nature, composed of both the dense and the subtle, and to use our capacity for reflection to elevate ourselves towards the purest essence of our being.

This premise speaks to us about the importance of balance and integration in our lives. It reminds us that it is necessary to connect with both the spiritual and the material, and to find a point of harmony between the two. In our daily life, this means seeking moments of introspection and connection with our spirituality, while actively engaging in the world and attending to our earthly responsibilities. It urges us to find a balance between internal growth and participation in the external world.

9. "Sic habebis gloriam totius mundi"

"Thus, you will have the glory of the whole world".

In the ninth sentence, the ascending and descending path of the human spirit is presented to us. It invites us to rise from the earth to the heavens, connecting with the divine and the transcendent, and then descend again to the earth, bringing with us the strength and power of the higher and the lower. This constant flow between the celestial and terrestrial realms allows us to evolve and grow, exchanging knowledge and experiences with the divine and the human. In this sense, we are urged to cultivate a spiritual life in harmony with our own beliefs and capabilities, seeking a balance that allows us to better adapt to our daily reality and relate harmoniously with others. By drawing the best from the spiritual and the material, without harming either our own being or the nature that surrounds us, we can nourish and develop all dimensions of our being: body, mind, soul, and spirit.

This premise speaks to us about the possibility of experiencing fulfillment and greatness in our life. It reminds us that by living in harmony with ourselves and the universe, we can experience glory and fullness that transcends individual limits. In our everyday life, this invites us to seek excellence in everything we do, to live with integrity and authenticity, and to positively contribute to the world around us. It inspires us to pursue our passions and purposes with determination and confidence, and to cultivate meaningful relationships and connections with others.

10. "Ideo fugiet a te omnis obscuritas"

"Therefore, all darkness will flee from you".

The tenth sentence reveals to us that by following these principles, we will achieve glory and banish all darkness. The glory here is not about fame or material wealth, but about gaining the knowledge that frees us and provides a profound understanding of reality. This knowledge gives us wings to fly through the realms of wisdom and gives us the freedom to make informed and transcendent decisions in our life. By obtaining this knowledge, we move away from ignorance and darkness, and become conscious and awakened beings. The light of wisdom dispels the shadows of ignorance, illuminating our path and guiding us towards a deeper understanding of ourselves and the world around us. By acquiring this knowledge, we are able to make more accurate decisions aligned with our true essence, avoiding the pitfalls of confusion and deception.

This premise speaks to us about the importance of inner light and knowledge in our life. It reminds us that by seeking wisdom and understanding, we can dispel darkness and overcome the obstacles that stand in our way. In our daily life, this impels us to cultivate the mind and spirit, to nourish ourselves with knowledge and wisdom, and to be aware of our limiting beliefs and thought patterns. It urges us to face our fears and limitations with courage and determination, knowing that the light of truth and knowledge will guide us on the path towards growth and personal fulfillment.

11. "Haec est totius fortitudinis fortitudo fortis, quia vincet omnem rem subtilem, omnemque solidam penetrabit"

"This is the strength of all strengths, for it will overcome everything subtle and penetrate everything solid".

In the eleventh sentence, we are presented with a supreme force, a force that transcends all others. It is a force that has the power to overcome any obstacle and to penetrate into the deepest matter. This force originates in the unfathomable, in the unknown. Although we cannot master or fully understand it, we can harness and use it on our path. It is a force in which we live and move, it is the very essence of our existence. This sentence invites us to recognize that there is a mysterious and powerful force that flows through us and all things, and that we can tune into it to achieve astonishing results. By recognizing and utilizing this greater force, we can overcome challenges and reach deeper levels of understanding and realization.

This premise speaks to us of the power and strength that lie within us. It reminds us that we have the capacity to overcome challenges and transcend apparent limits. In our daily life, this motivates us to develop inner strength, to face obstacles with determination, and to cultivate a resilient mindset. It urges us to believe in our own ability to overcome and to trust in our power to transform circumstances and achieve our goals.

12. "Sic mundus creatus est"

"So the world was created".

In this twelfth affirmation, it is revealed to us that all the teachings and principles previously set forth are the very foundations of the creation of the world. It is through the supreme and omnipresent force that modulates and materializes the subtle and the dense, that the finite and changing universe arises from the orbit of the Absolute. This relative universe is the stage on which we exist, and each one of us is a particle that contains within itself the keys to create and recreate other universes. It is an affirmation that invites us to recognize our intimate connection with the cosmos and to assume our responsibility as co-creators of our own reality.

This premise speaks to us of a vision of a world created according to universal principles and divine laws. It reminds us that existence itself reflects a higher intention and purpose. In our daily life, this invites us to appreciate the beauty and harmony of the world around us, to recognize our connection with the cosmos, and to be aware of our role in the co-creation of our reality. It encourages us to live in harmony with nature and to honor the interdependence among all living beings.

13. "Hinc erunt adaptationes mirabiles, quarum modus est hic"

"From here will come amazing adaptations, the method of which is here".

The thirteenth sentence speaks to us of the infinite possibilities of adaptation and transformation that arise from understanding the previous teachings. As we explore the world we live in, we discover incredible applications and realities that allow us to advance in all aspects of life. Science, technology, and spirituality constantly reveal to us new ways to adapt and harness what we already know to reach the unknown. It is important to remember that there is not just one path to access knowledge, and each person can find their own way to understanding. However, it is essential to maintain a critical attitude and to discern between what is beneficial and what is not, using our common sense as a guide on our journey of exploration and discovery.

This premise speaks to us about the capacity for adaptation and transformation that resides within us. It reminds us that we can learn and grow from the circumstances and challenges we face in life. It urges us to seize opportunities for change and evolution to create wonderful outcomes. In our daily life, this encourages us to embrace challenges as opportunities for growth and to be flexible in our way of thinking and acting. It invites us to seek creative solutions and to adapt to changing circumstances with ingenuity and openness. It reminds us that the path to success and fulfillment is full of adaptations and transformations that allow us to flourish and reach our maximum potential.

14. "Itaque vocatus sum Hermes Trismegistus, habens tres partes philosophiae totius mundi"

"Therefore, I was called Hermes Trismegistus, possessing the three parts of the philosophy of the whole world".

In the fourteenth and final sentence of the Emerald Tablet, Hermes Trismegistus claims to have possessed the three fundamental parts of universal philosophy. These three parts refer to the broad fields of ancient knowledge, such as astrology, philosophy, and mastery in various disciplines. Hermes Trismegistus, as the holder of this vast knowledge, is called the 'Thrice Great.' Referring to the operation of the sun, he indicates that what he had previously affirmed has been fulfilled and concluded. His words have brought the light of knowledge to dispel doubts, affirm truths, and provide guidance to those who study and apply his teachings. Hermes Trismegistus, aware of the importance of adaptation and transformation, leaves his legacy for future generations to continue seeking a bright future, turning darkness into light and the corruptible into incorruptible. Each human soul has the potential to transform, revealing the subtlety and brilliance of the gold that lies within.

This premise speaks to us about the synthesis and integration of knowledge and wisdom. It shows us the totality of philosophy and knowledge that encompasses all areas of existence. In our daily lives, this invites us to seek a holistic and balanced approach in our quest for knowledge and understanding. It inspires us to explore different disciplines and perspectives, and to seek the connection between them to gain a more complete and profound view of the world. It reminds us that learning and acquiring wisdom is an ongoing journey that spans multiple areas of life and helps us develop a broader understanding of ourselves and the world we live in.

These propositions, extracted from the T*abula Smaragdina* or *Emerald Tablet*, contain ancestral wisdom and invite us to reflect on our life and our role in the world. By integrating these principles into our daily lives, we can cultivate a greater sense of connection, wisdom, and fulfillment.

> "The Emerald Tablet contains the foundations of Hermetic philosophy and is considered one of the most important texts in the study of alchemy. In it are found the universal principles of transmutation and the unity of the macrocosm and the microcosm."
>
> *Manly P. Hall:*

ABOUT HERMES TRISMEGISTUS

"Hermes Trismegistus is a mythical figure that embodies divine wisdom. He is attributed with the writing of sacred books that contain the essence of universal knowledge. During my expedition in Egypt, I sought his teachings and was deeply inspired by his legacy".

Alejandro Magno

Hermes Trismegistus, known as the "Thrice Great", is an enigmatic and revered figure in Hermetic tradition. His legacy spans across history, and he is credited with profound wisdom and spiritual knowledge. Said to be an ancient master and guide, he lived in ancient Egypt during a period when humanity was in its infancy. He is considered the Great Central Sun of Occultism, a divine messenger who received and imparted sacred teachings.

A contemporary of Abraham, and possibly even his instructor; Hermes Trismegistus left an invaluable legacy through Hermetic teachings. These teachings form the foundation of numerous esoteric and philosophical traditions, influencing the understanding of reality and human nature.

Hermes is known for his writings and treatises –among them the foundations of T*he Kybalion*– addressing a wide range of topics, including alchemy, astrology, philosophy, magic, and connection to the divine. His teachings delve into universal principles, revealing the laws governing the cosmos and the potential for human inner transformation. His figure has been revered as a spiritual guide and beacon of wisdom throughout the centuries. His teachings have been preserved and passed down by generations of truth seekers, and his influence has permeated different cultures and traditions around the world. His legacy invites us to explore the mysteries of existence, to cultivate inner wisdom, and to seek a deeper understanding of our purpose in the universe.

Ultimately, the figure of Hermes Trismegistus reminds us that spiritual knowledge transcends the barriers of time and space, and that eternal wisdom is available to those who sincerely seek. As a guide and teacher, he continues to inspire restless souls and truth seekers to embark on the path of self discovery and spiritual enlightenment.

THE KYBALION

—"My dear Alice, in the gardens of memory, in the palace of dreams.
That is where you and I shall meet.
—But a dream isn't reality!
—Who's to say which is which?"

Alice in Wonderland

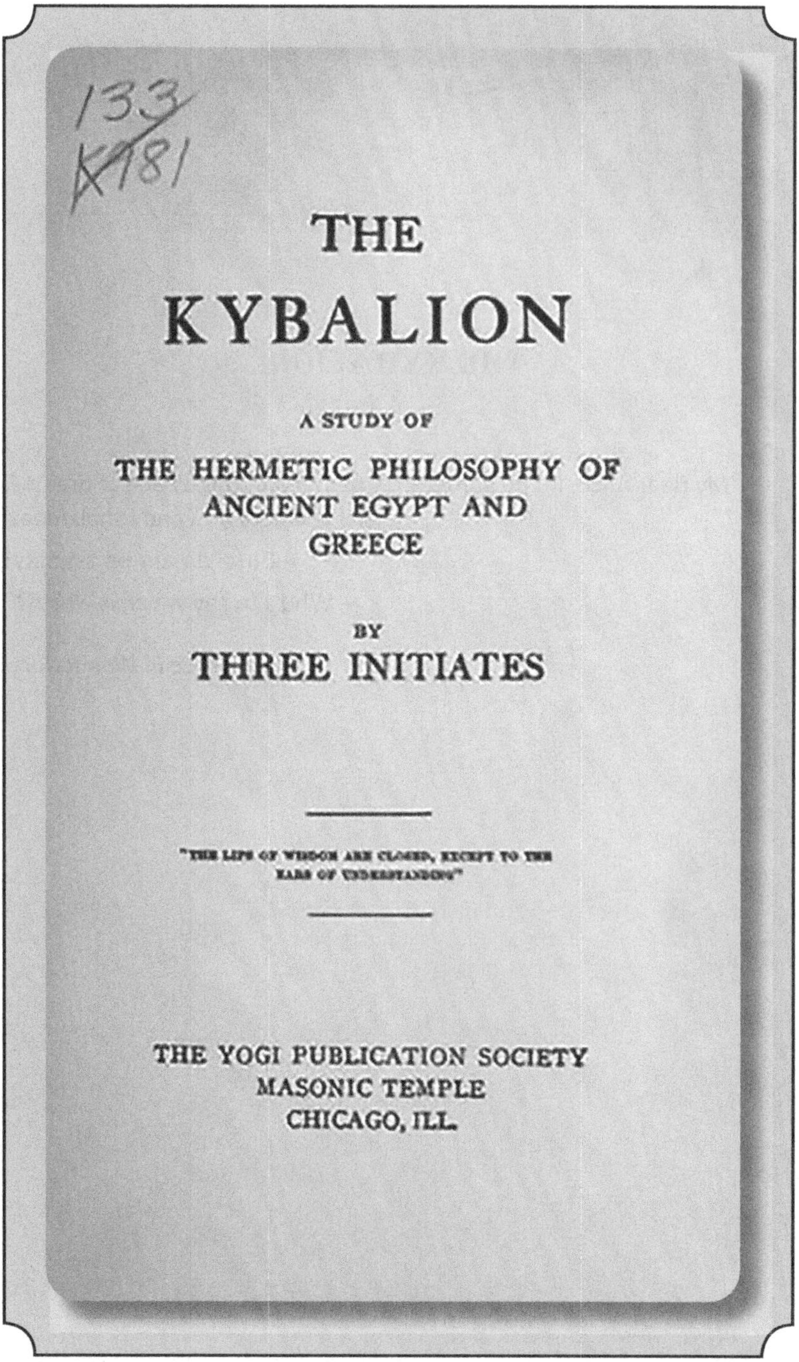

THE KYBALION

A STUDY OF

THE HERMETIC PHILOSOPHY OF ANCIENT EGYPT AND GREECE

BY

THREE INITIATES

"THE LIPS OF WISDOM ARE CLOSED, EXCEPT TO THE EARS OF UNDERSTANDING"

THE YOGI PUBLICATION SOCIETY
MASONIC TEMPLE
CHICAGO, ILL.

INTRODUCTION

We are greatly pleased to present this work to the students and researchers of the Secret Doctrines[1]. This work is rooted in the ancient Hermetic teachings, and its scarce —or nonexistent— reflection in the literary field is surprising. Although numerous references have been made throughout occultist writings, very little has been said about this particular subject. However, those researchers of hidden truths have undoubtedly sensed the arrival of this book.

The purpose of this work does not lie in the proclamation of a specific philosophy or doctrine, but rather in providing the student with an exegesis of the truth that allows them to reconcile the multiple aspects of the occult knowledge they have already acquired. Often, these pieces of knowledge seem contradictory and paradoxical, which can discourage and displease the beginner. Our goal is not to build a new temple of wisdom, but to place in the hands of the researcher a master key with which they can open the numerous inner doors that lead to the Temple of Mystery[2].

No occult knowledge has been so zealously guarded as the fragments of the Hermetic teachings. These valuable legacies have endured throughout the centuries since the times of the Great

---

1 The 'Secret Doctrines' are often transmitted through traditions and esoteric knowledge systems that have been maintained over the centuries, passing from masters to select students in a continuous line of teaching. These teachings are often wrapped in allegories, symbolism, and coded language, intended to protect and preserve their integrity and to keep them away from those who are not prepared to receive them or who might misinterpret them

2 "The 'Temple of Mystery' represents a state of expanded consciousness and the quest for spiritual truth beyond the veils of illusion. It is the place where one delves into the mysteries of the universe and oneself, on a journey of self discovery and spiritual transcendence".

Founder, Hermes Trismegistus, "the chosen of the gods", whose life extinguished in ancient Egypt, when humanity as a whole was still a child in development. In that era, Hermes shared his existence with notable figures such as Abraham, and if the legend does not deceive us, even instructed the venerable sage. Hermes was and continues to be the Central Sun of Occultism, whose rays have illuminated every corner of knowledge that has been transmitted since then.

All the fundamental bases of the esoteric teachings that have been imparted to humanity have their origin, essentially, in those formulated by Hermes. Even the most ancient doctrines of India have their source in the Hermetic teachings. These profound truths have flowed through time and space, shaping the beliefs and knowledge of numerous cultures.

From the sacred land of the Ganges, many advanced occultists embarked on a journey to Egypt to pay homage to the Master. There they found the key that, while providing explanations, harmonized their diverse viewpoints, thus solidly establishing the Secret Doctrine. Disciples and novices arrived from all corners of the world, recognizing Hermes as the Master of Masters. His influence was so profound that, despite the denials of countless instructors in different countries, it is evident to find in the teachings of these latter the essential foundations of the Hermetic doctrines.

The student of comparative religions can easily perceive the immense influence that the Hermetic teachings have exerted on all beliefs, regardless of the names under which they are known today, whether ancient religions or those that endure in the present. The analogy is striking, despite the apparent contradictions, and the Hermetic teachings act as a mediator between them, unifying their different elements.

The work of Hermes appears to have been oriented towards sowing a great truth, which has grown and flourished in such diverse and unique forms, rather than establishing a philosophical school that governed the thought of the world. Nonetheless, the original truth taught by him has been kept intact, in its primordial purity, by a select group of individuals in each era. These men, rejecting numerous enthusiasts and underdeveloped students, followed the Hermetic principles and reserved their knowledge for those few who were ready to understand and master it. Among these chosen ones, the knowledge was transmitted orally, in an intimate circle of trust.

Throughout generations and in various regions of the world, there have always been initiates who have kept the sacred flame of the Hermetic teachings alive. These men have always longed to use their lamps to ignite the smaller flames of those in the profane world, when the light of truth weakened and clouded due to negligence, or when the wick became soiled with foreign elements. There have always been those few who have cared for the altar of truth, perpetually keeping the lamp of Wisdom lit. These men have dedicated their lives to this noble task of love, described by the poet in these verses:

"Oh, do not let the flame die out! Cherished age after age in its dark cavern, in its holy temples cherished. Fed by pure ministers of love, do not let the flame die out![3]"

These men never sought popular approval nor longed to accumulate a large number of followers. They are indifferent to such things, for they know in advance how few there are in each generation capable of receiving and recognizing the truth if it were presented to them. They reserve the meat for the men while others

---

3 "With eternal zeal, they fulfill their mission of fire, igniting hearts in darkness, and protecting the altar where Truth rests, burning with the flame of Wisdom"

give milk to the children. They guard their pearls of wisdom for the few chosen who can appreciate their value and carry them in their crowns, instead of casting them before pigs who would sully and trample them in the mire of their pigsties.

However, these men have not forgotten the precepts of Hermes regarding the transmission of these teachings to those who are prepared to receive them. As The Kybalion states: "Wherever the footprints of the Master are found, the ears of those ready to receive his teachings open wide". Additionally, it adds: "When the ear is ready to listen, then the lips come to fill it with wisdom". But their attitude has always been in strict accordance with another aphorism from The Kybalion, which maintains that "the lips of Wisdom remain closed, except to the ear capable of understanding.

And it is precisely those ears incapable of understanding that have criticized this attitude of the Hermetists and have publicly lamented that they have never clearly expressed the true spirit of their teachings, without reservations or reticence. However, a retrospective look at the pages of history will reveal the wisdom of the masters, who knew the folly of trying to teach the world what it neither desired nor was prepared to receive. The Hermetists have never sought to be martyrs, but instead, have remained withdrawn, silent, and smiling at the efforts of those who, in their fervent enthusiasm, believed they could impose truths on an uncivilized humanity that can only be understood by those who have advanced far on the path.

The spirit of persecution still persists on Earth. There are certain Hermetic teachings that, if divulged, would attract a clamor of hatred and the contempt of the masses upon their disseminators, who would again cry out: "Crucify him!.. Crucify him!".

In this small book, we have tried to give you an idea of the fundamental teachings of The Kybalion, pointing out everything related to the current principles, leaving you the task of studying them in depth, rather than addressing them in detail ourselves. If you are true students or disciples, you will understand and be able to apply these principles; otherwise, you must develop them, as otherwise the Hermetic teachings will be nothing but "words, words, words" to you.

The Three Initiates

CHAPTER I

THE HERMETIC PHILOSOPHY

"The lips of wisdom are closed, except to the ears of understanding".
The Kybalion.

From ancient times, the ancestral legacy of ancient Egypt has spread its primal and secret teachings, exerting a powerful influence over the philosophical systems of all races and peoples throughout entire centuries. The homeland of the majestic pyramids and the enigmatic Sphinx, Egypt, served as the cradle of Occult Wisdom and mystical doctrines. Every nation has drawn its own from these esoteric teachings: India, Persia, Chaldea, Media, China, Japan, Assyria, ancient Greece and Rome, and other countries of equal importance have generously availed them selves of the doctrines formulated by the wise hierophants[4] and masters

4 Hierophant: From Latin "hierophantes", and this from Greek "ἱεροφάντης" (hierophántēs).
1. n. Priest of Eleusis in Greece, who presided over the celebration of sacred mysteries.
2. n. Teacher of esoteric knowledge or hidden truths.

of the land of Isis[5]. These teachings were exclusively transmitted to those who were prepared to delve into the hidden mysteries.

It was in ancient Egypt where extraordinary beings, adepts and masters of incomparable greatness, flourished, whose excellence has rarely been equaled in the centuries that have passed since the times of the Great Hermes. Egypt housed the prestigious Great Lodge of mystical fraternities. Through the doors of its temples entered the neophytes, who, upon becoming adepts, hierophants, and masters, dispersed everywhere, carrying with them the valuable knowledge they possessed and longing to share it with those prepared to receive it. No student of occultism can deny the enormous debt owed to those venerable masters of Egypt, whose legacy lives on in our teachings to this day.

However, among those illustrious masters, there stood one who was acclaimed as "the Master of Masters". This being, if he can be classified as "human", dwelled in ancient Egypt during immemorial times and was known by the name of Hermes Trismegistus. His wisdom transcended the limits of the ordinary, granting him a divine status in the history of humanity.

He was the father of wisdom, the visionary who laid the foundations of astrology and unveiled the secrets of alchemy. The details of his existence have faded into the folds of history, swept away by the vast temporal abyss that separates us from those times. The precise date of his birth in ancient Egypt, in his last manifestation on this earthly plane, is lost in the mists of unknowing. However, it is rumored that he was contemporary with the most ancient dynasties

---

5 Isis was an Egyptian deity, considered the mother goddess of magic, fertility, and protection. She was the wife of Osiris and the mother of Horus, playing a crucial role in Osiris's resurrection and battling Seth to secure the throne of Egypt for her son. Worshiped throughout ancient Egypt and beyond, she represented feminine power and divine wisdom and was sought after for assistance in areas such as motherhood and magic. Her legacy in Egyptian mythology and culture is enduring

of Egypt, long before the time of Moses. The most learned scholars in the field maintain that he lived in the same era as Abraham, and in some Jewish traditions, it is daringly asserted that Abraham acquired much of his knowledge directly from Hermes himself.

After numerous years passed since his death (it is said that he lived three hundred years), the Egyptians elevated him to the status of divinity and worshiped him as one of their gods, under the name of Thoth. In time, the Greeks also consecrated him as one of their deities, bestowing upon him the title of "Hermes, the god of wisdom". Both the Greeks and the Egyptians honored his memory over the centuries, calling him the "enlightened by the gods" and adding to his ancient name the epithet "Trismegistus", which means "thrice great". These ancient civilizations venerated him, and his name became synonymous with "source of wisdom".

Even today, we use the term "hermetic" to refer to something that is "secret" or "reserved", and this is because the followers of Hermeticism have always zealously guarded the mystery of their teachings. Although at that time the expression "do not cast pearls before swine" was not known, they followed a special code of conduct that indicated "give milk to the children and meat to the men", maxims that are familiar to all those who have read the biblical scriptures. It is worth noting that these maxims had already been used many centuries before the Christian Era[6].

---

6 The expression "give milk to children and meat to men" is not a direct biblical reference. However, it is a phrase that evokes an idea present in various traditions and scriptures, including the Bible. This phrase is a metaphor that represents the idea of providing teachings that are appropriate and understandable according to each individual's capacity for understanding. In the biblical context, we could relate it to passages such as 1 Corinthians 3:2, where it is mentioned that initially, basic teaching, like milk, is given to new believers, and then they are fed with deeper teaching, like meat, as they mature in their faith. Although it is not a direct quotation from the Bible, the idea of giving milk to children and meat to men is consistent with principles found in biblical teachings

This strategy of cautiously spreading the truth has been a constant among the Hermetists, even in our times. The Hermetic teachings are found in every corner of the world and in all religions, without being identified with any particular country or community. This is due to the preaching of the ancient instructors, who sought to prevent the Secret Doctrine from crystallizing into a creed. The wisdom of this measure is evident to any student of history. The ancient occultism of India and Persia deteriorated and their knowledge was lost, because the instructors became priests and mixed theology with philosophy. As a result, their wisdom transformed into a vast array of religious superstitions, cults, creeds, and deities.

The same happened with the Hermetic teachings of the Christian Gnostics[7], which were lost during the era of Constantine. He tainted the philosophy by mixing it with theology, and the Christian church lost its true essence and spirit. For several centuries, it was forced to wander in darkness, unable to find its way. Even today, it is observed how the Christian church struggles to return to its ancient mystical teachings, trying to rediscover its lost path.

Throughout time, a few souls have kept the flame alive, tending to it carefully and ensuring that its light did not go out. Thanks to those steadfast hearts and minds of extraordinary development, we still possess the truth among us. However, it is not found in books. It has been transmitted from Master to disciple, from initiate to neophyte, whispered from lips to ears. If anything has ever

---

7 The Christian Gnostics were a religious and philosophical group in the early centuries of Christianity who considered themselves bearers of secret spiritual knowledge. They interpreted Christian texts through their Gnostic approach, emphasizing the importance of spiritual revelation and direct knowledge of God. They viewed the material world as imperfect and controlled by evil forces and believed in a cosmic dualism. Although considered heretics by mainstream Christianity, their legacy and writings have been the subject of study and interest in the history of Christianity and Gnostic thought

been written about it, its meaning has been carefully disguised under the veils of astrology and alchemy, in such a way that only those who possessed the key could decipher it correctly. This was necessary to avoid the persecutions of the theologians of the Middle Ages, who fought against the Secret Doctrine with ferocity. Although nowadays we can still find some valuable books of Hermetic philosophy, most have been lost over time. However, the Hermetic Philosophy is the only master key capable of opening the doors to all hidden knowledge.

In ancient times, there existed a compilation of certain Hermetic doctrines that served as the foundations of the entire Secret Doctrine. These teachings had been transmitted from instructor to student, and this compilation was known as The Kybalion, whose true meaning was lost for hundreds of years. Nevertheless, some fortunate individuals who received these maxims directly from lips to ears understand and know them in their essence. These precepts had never been written until now. They are simply a series of maxims and axioms that the Initiates were responsible for explaining and expanding. These teachings represent the fundamental principles of "Hermetic alchemy", which, contrary to common belief, is based on the mastery of mental forces rather than material elements. It is about the transmutation of mental vibrations, rather than the conversion of metals. The legend surrounding the philosopher's stone, which transformed metals into gold, was an allegory related to Hermetic Philosophy, an allegory that was perfectly understood by the disciples of authentic Hermeticism.

In this modest work, we extend an invitation to our students to explore the Hermetic teachings as they were presented in *The Kybalion*. We, mere apprentices of these teachings, though bearing the title of initiates, are humble disciples prostrated at the feet of Hermes, the Great Master. Here we transcribe numerous maxims and precepts from The Kybalion, accompanied by explanations and comments that we believe will serve to facilitate the understanding of these teachings by modern men. It is important to bear in mind that the original text has been intentionally veiled with obscure and perplexing terms, but we trust that our explanations will shed light on its meaning.

The original maxims, axioms, and precepts of The Kybalion are presented in a distinct typography in these pages. We wish for the readers of this book to obtain valuable knowledge from the study of its pages, just like those who have traveled the path towards mastery since the times of Hermes Trismegistus, the Master of Masters, the Enlightened, up to the present day.

Says The Kybalion:

> *"Wherever the footprints of the Master are found, the ears of the one who is ready to receive his teachings open wide".*
>
> *"When the ear is prepared to listen, then come the lips that will fill it with wisdom".*

Thus, in accordance with what is established, this book will only capture the attention of those who are ready to receive it. And in turn, when the student is prepared to receive the truth, then this book will come to him. The Hermetic principle of cause and effect, in its manifestation as the "law of attraction", will draw the ears to the lips and the book to the disciple in perfect harmony.

"When the thinking mind remains calm, you observe reality as it is, all aspects together: the tree, the sky, and the Earth, the rain and the stars are not separate. Life and death, the Self and the Other are not separate; just as the mountain and the valley are inseparable".

CHAPTER II

THE SEVEN HERMETIC PRINCIPLES

In the realms of truth, seven principles enlighten the wise who understand them, granting them the magical key that unveils a threshold where the doors of the Temple unfold wide open.

The Kybalion

The Hermetic Philosophy is based on seven immutable principles:

1. The Principle of Mentalism.
2. The Principle of Correspondence.
3. The Principle of Vibration.
4. The Principle of Polarity.
5. The Principle of Rhythm.
6. The Principle of Cause and Effect.
7. The Principle of Generation.

THE PRINCIPLE OF MENTALISM

"The ALL is Mind; the universe is mental".
The Kybalion.

This principle reveals the essence of "everything is mind". It explains that the ALL, the real substance hidden behind every manifestation and appearance we know as the "material world", "phenomena of life", "matter", "energy", and everything we perceive through our senses, is actually spirit. A spirit that in itself is unknowable and indefinable, but that we can consider as an infinite, universal, and living mind. Moreover, it shows us that the phenomenal world, the universe itself, is a mental creation of the ALL, a projection in the mind in which we live, move, and exist.

This axiom, by affirming the mental nature of the universe, provides a simple explanation for the various mental and psychic phenomena that have captured public attention and defy any scientific hypothesis without this understanding. By understanding this Hermetic principle of mentalism, the individual acquires the ability to comprehend and apply the laws governing the mental universe for their own wellbeing and development. The student of Hermetic Philosophy can consciously employ the powerful mental laws, instead of depending on them accidentally or being manipulated by their influence. With this master key in their possession, the disciple can open the doors of the temple of mental and psychic knowledge, entering with freedom and intelligence.

This principle offers us a profound understanding of the true nature of energy, force, and matter, as well as how and why they are subject to the dominion of the mind. A long time ago, an ancient Master wrote: "Whoever understands the truth that the universe is mental, has advanced much on the path of mastery". And these words remain just as true today as they were when they were written. Without this fundamental key, mastery is unattainable, and the student who lacks it will knock in vain at the door of the Temple and will not be received.

THE PRINCIPLE OF CORRESPONDENCE

"As above, so below; as below, so above".

The Kybalion.

This principle embodies the truth that there is always a correspondence between the laws and phenomena across the various states of being and life. The ancient Hermetic axiom states precisely: *"As above, so below; as below, so above"*. By understanding this principle, one gains a key to solving many of the enigmas and paradoxes that contain the mysterious secrets of Nature. Although there are planes unknown to us, by applying this law of correspondence to them, much of what would otherwise be incomprehensible gains clarity in our consciousness. This law has universal application across the various levels of the *Kosmos*[8], whether mental, material, or spiritual: it is a law that transcends all boundaries.

---

8 In "The Kybalion", the term "Kosmos" refers to the universe in its entirety, understood as an orderly and harmonious system of all manifestations of reality. The Kybalion is a hermetic text that presents philosophical and esoteric principles, and it uses the term "Kosmos" to denote the entirety of everything that exists, both in the material and in the mental and spiritual realms. It is considered that the Kosmos is governed by universal laws, and that everything within it is interconnected and related. It is a holistic and transcendent view of reality, encompassing everything from galaxies and stars to subatomic particles, as well as the subtlest aspects of consciousness and spirit.

The ancient Hermetists regarded this principle as one of the most valuable allies of the mind, for through it, the veil hiding the unknown from our lives could be drawn aside. Its application could partly tear the Veil of Isis[9], allowing us, albeit fleetingly, to glimpse some of the attributes of the goddess. Just as understanding the principles of geometry enables a man to measure the diameter, orbit, and movement of the most distant stars while seated in his observatory, so too does the knowledge of the principle of correspondence allow a man to reason intelligently about the known and the unknown; by studying the monad, one comes to understand the archangel[10].

9 The "Veil of Isis" is a metaphor used in esoteric and symbolic contexts to represent the mystery and veil of hidden and profound knowledge. In Egyptian mythology, Isis was a goddess associated with wisdom and divine secrets. The veil symbolizes that which is concealed and protected from direct view, the unknown, and the inaccessible to the common human mind. Tearing the "Veil of Isis" implies reaching a deeper level of knowledge and understanding, unveiling the secrets and transcendental truths that lie beyond the obvious. It is a symbol of the pursuit of spiritual wisdom and the desire to transcend the boundaries of tangible reality in the search for ultimate truth

10 "Studying the monad leads to understanding the archangel" implies that by delving into the knowledge and understanding of the monad, which in philosophy refers to the indivisible and essential unity of being, one can attain a higher and more comprehensive understanding of the archangel. The monad represents the purest and most fundamental essence of an individual or entity, while the archangel refers to a high ranking and powerful spiritual figure in many religious and esoteric traditions. Therefore, the phrase suggests that by studying and exploring the nature and deeper essence of oneself or existence, one can gain a more complete and enlightening perspective on divine entities and their role in the cosmic order.

THE PRINCIPLE OF VIBRATION

"Nothing rests; everything moves; everything vibrates".
The Kybalion

This principle embodies the dynamic truth that everything is in constant motion, that nothing remains still, a truth that is confirmed and supported by modern science with each new discovery. Yet, it is astonishing to think that this Hermetic principle was stated centuries ago by the wise Masters of ancient Egypt. This teaching reveals the differences between the various manifestations of matter, force, mind, and even spirit, which are merely the result of varied vibratory states. From the ALL, which represents pure spirit, to the densest form of matter, everything is in constant vibration. The higher the vibration, the higher its position on the scale. The vibration of the spirit is of such intense infinity, so powerful that it almost appears to be at rest, in the same way that a wheel spinning at high speed appears motionless. On the other end of the scale, there are forms of extremely dense matter whose vibration is so weak that it also seems to be at rest. Between these two poles, there are countless degrees of vibratory intensity. From subatomic particles and electrons to atoms, molecules, stars, and entire universes, everything is in vibration. This principle is equally applicable to states or planes of energy or force (which are nothing but particular vibratory states) and to the mental and spiritual planes. A complete understanding of this principle gives the Hermetic student the power to control their own mental vibrations, as well as those of others. The Masters also use this principle to conquer natural phenomena. "He who understands the vibratory principle has grasped the scepter of power", said one of the ancient writers with undying wisdom.

THE PRINCIPLE OF POLARITY

> "Everything is dual; everything has two poles; everything has its pair of opposites: like and unlike are the same; opposites are identical in nature, but different in degree; extremes meet; all truths are but half truths; all paradoxes may be reconciled".
>
> *The Kybalion.*

In this vast universe, every aspect possesses its inseparable opposite, as duality permeates existence. Like and unlike are interwoven in an endless dance, revealing their intrinsic connection. Opposites, though sharing the same essence, differ in degree. Extremes converge in an unexpected meeting, where they touch and intertwine. All truths, in their essence, are half truths, and all paradoxes have the capacity to find reconciliation. In this eternal flow of contrasts, the deep interconnection that transcends apparent contradictions is revealed, inviting us to explore the vastness of reality and discover the underlying harmony that unites all aspects of existence.

This principle embodies the truth of duality inherent in all existence: every aspect has its counterpart, every element its pair of opposites. These statements, originating from ancient Hermetic axioms, shed light on the paradoxes that have baffled countless researchers over time. These paradoxes maintain that thesis and antithesis are identical in nature, differing only in degree; that opposites are, in reality, identical but with different levels of manifestation; that extremes can unite and that each truth is only a half truth. This principle teaches us that in everything there are two poles, two aspects, and that opposites are simply the extremes of the same entity, differing in their degree of manifestation. Heat and cold, though opposite in appearance, are essentially the same substance, varying only in intensity. Contemplate a thermometer and try to discern where heat begins and cold ends. There is no point of absolute heat in itself; both terms, cold and heat, represent different degrees of the same entity, a manifestation of the principle of polarity we are discussing

This principle is equally manifested in light and darkness, which, in essence, are a single entity that varies in degrees between the two poles of the phenomenon. Where does darkness end and light begin? What is the difference between large and small, hard and soft, white and black, high and low, positive and negative? The paradox is clarified through the principle of polarity. This same principle operates on the mental plane. Take, for example, love and hate, two seemingly opposite mental states, but in reality, they have many intermediate degrees. So many, in fact, that the words we use to describe them, "pleasant" and "unpleasant", fade into each other, to the point where it is often difficult to discern whether something gives us pleasure or displeasure. They are, in essence, different levels of the same reality, as you will understand upon reflection. Moreover, it is possible to change or transmute the vibrations of hate into vibrations of love, both in our own mind and in the minds of others. This is considered of utmost importance by the Hermetists. Many of those reading these words have experienced in themselves and others the rapid and sometimes involuntary transition from love to hate and vice versa. Now you will understand the possibility of effecting this transmutation through the power of will, following Hermetic formulas.

"Good" and "evil" are simply the poles of the same reality. The Hermetist understands and masters the art of transmuting evil into good through the intelligent application of the principle of polarity. In summary, the "art of polarizing" becomes a phase of mental alchemy, practiced and mastered by both ancient and modern Hermetic Masters. Perfect understanding of this principle enables the individual to change their own polarity, as well as that of others, if they dedicate the necessary time and study to master this art. It is through the knowledge and conscious application of polarity that the secrets of mental alchemy are revealed, allowing the transformation of negative energies into positive, darkness into light, and evil into good. It is a powerful tool for personal development and spiritual transmutation, giving the Hermetist mastery over their own internal reality and the ability to influence the world around them. In the ceaseless dance of opposing poles lies the potential for growth, transformation, and the manifestation of the fullness of being.

THE PRINCIPLE OF RHYTHM

> "Everything flows and ebbs; everything has periods of advancement and retreat, everything rises and falls; everything swings like a pendulum; the extent of its movement to the right is the same as its movement to the left; rhythm is the compensation".
>
> *The Kybalion.*

In this vast symphony of existence, everything flows and moves in a constant ebb and flow. Every aspect has its moments of advancement and retreat, of ascent and descent. Life itself resembles a pendulum swinging in its ceaseless dance. The movement to the right finds its perfect counterpart in the movement to the left, and in this harmony of opposites, rhythm becomes the sublime compensation. Everything in the universe is imbued with this divine beat, where every action is followed by its reaction, every rise by its fall. It is in this constant flow, in this eternal back and forth, where balance and harmony are found, inviting us to tune our hearts to the cosmic pulse that surrounds us.

This principle embraces the truth that everything manifests in a constant swing, in a flow and ebb, in the oscillation of a pendulum that moves between the two poles according to the principle of polarity, described just a moment ago. There is always action and reaction, advance and retreat, rise and fall. This law rules in all aspects: in suns, in worlds, in animals, in the mind, in energy, in matter. This law manifests itself both in the creation and destruction of worlds, in the progress and decline of nations, in life and in all things. But it is in the mental states of human beings where the hermetists believe this principle acquires its greatest importance

The hermetists have discovered this principle and have found its universal application, and they have also discovered certain methods to escape its effects by using the appropriate formulas and techniques. They employ the mental law of neutralization. They cannot annul the principle or prevent it from operating, but they have learned to evade its effects to a certain degree, a degree that depends on their mastery of this principle. They know how to use it instead of being used by it. It is in this, and in other similar methods, where the hermetic science lies. The Master polarizes himself at the point where he wishes to remain, thus neutralizing the rhythmic oscillation of the pendulum that would drag him to the other pole. All those who have acquired a certain degree of self mastery do this to some extent, either consciously or unconsciously, but the Master does it consciously and, by the power of his will, achieves a level of mental stability and firmness that is almost incomprehensible to the great multitude that fluctuates in a continuous wavelike motion, driven by the principle of rhythm. This principle, like that of polarity, has been thoroughly studied by the hermetists, and the methods to counteract, neutralize, and employ them constitute one of the most fundamental parts of hermetic mental alchemy.

THE PRINCIPLE OF CAUSE AND EFFECT

> "Every Cause has its Effect; every Effect has its Cause; everything happens according to Law; Chance is but a name for Law not recognized; there are many planes of causality, but nothing escapes the Law".
>
> *The Kybalion.*

Every action has its reaction, every consequence has its origin, everything happens in conformity with an immutable law. Luck is nothing but a label given to that law which is not fully recognized. There may be multiple planes of apparent chance, but nothing escapes the influence of the Law. In this vast fabric of existence, every cause triggers an effect, and every effect has its roots in a cause. It is a cosmic game of cause and effect, where each movement is guided by invisible threads of order and balance. Luck, simply, is the veil that hides the deep understanding of the laws governing the universe. Although there may be moments of apparent randomness, each event finds its place within the chains of cause and effect that intertwine in a cosmic dance. Nothing is outside the reach of the Law, not an atom nor a star, for everything is subject to the powerful forces that weave the tapestry of destiny.

This principle embodies the profound truth that in every event there is an underlying cause and in every cause, an effect is manifested. It powerfully explains that "Everything happens according to the Law"; that no event occurs simply by chance or without apparent reason; that there is no such thing as chance in the universal order. Although there are multiple planes of cause and effect that intertwine in a complex web, the higher planes exert a dominant influence over the lower ones, yet even amidst this hierarchy, nothing completely escapes the Law that governs the universe.

Those who have delved into the secrets of Hermetic wisdom have understood the art and methods of rising above the ordinary plane of cause and effect, to a certain degree. Through a mental elevation to a higher plane, these sages become the architects of their own reality, the conscious creators of their own destinies. While the masses are carried along by the current, blindly obeying their environment, the will and desires of those with greater power, their inheritance, suggestion, and other external causes, like pawns on the great chessboard of Life, the Masters have transcended this condition.

By elevating themselves to the higher plane, they have managed to master their states of mind, mold their characteristics and qualities, awaken their latent powers, and transform the environment around them. They become the architects of their own destiny, the protagonists of THE GREAT GAME OF LIFE. Their will stands like a beacon in the darkness, their vision penetrates the higher spheres, and their wisdom guides every step they take. Instead of being mere players, subject to external wills and circumstances, they use the Principle to their advantage. They have learned to be the conductors of universal energies, to tune in with the symphony of the cosmos, and to use the Law to manifest their highest desires and purposes. Although they obey the Causality of the higher planes in which they find themselves, they also actively contribute to governing their own plane of existence, carrying with them the torch of Hermetic knowledge and transmitting their wisdom to those who are prepared to receive it.

In this statement, an immense wealth of Hermetic knowledge is condensed, a wisdom that can only be expounded by those who are willing to read between the lines and explore the deepest mysteries of the universe. Those who embark on this quest with an open mind and receptive heart will be destined to discover the transcendence of the Universal Laws and become Masters of their own fate.

THE PRINCIPLE OF GENERATION

"Generation exists everywhere; everything has its masculine and feminine principles; generation manifests on all planes".

The Kybalion

This principle encapsulates the profound truth that generation is present in everything, with the masculine and feminine principles in constant action. This truth transcends not only the physical plane but also the mental and spiritual ones. In the physical world, this principle manifests as "sex", and on the higher planes, it takes more elevated forms, but its essence remains the same. No physical, mental, or spiritual creation is possible without this vital principle. Its understanding illuminates numerous enigmas that have puzzled the human mind. This creative principle is always operating in the sense of "generating", "regenerating", and "creating". Every human being contains within themselves both elements of this principle. If you aspire to unveil the philosophy of mental and spiritual creation, generation, and regeneration, you must study this Hermetic principle closely, as it holds the key to many mysteries of life.

However, we caution that this principle has no relation to the harmful and degrading theories, teachings, and practices promoted under sensational titles. These represent a prostitution of the great natural principle of generation. Such theories and practices are merely a resurrection of the ancient phallic doctrines, which can only lead to the ruin of the mind, soul, and body. The Hermetic Philosophy has always raised its voice in protest against these liberties and perversions of natural principles. If you seek such teachings, you must look elsewhere, for Hermeticism contains nothing related to them. To those who are pure of heart, all things are pure; to the corrupt, everything is corruption.

CHAPTER III

MENTAL TRANSMUTATION

> "The mind (like metals and elements) can be transmuted, from state to state; from degree to degree; from condition to condition; from pole to pole; from vibration to vibration. True Hermetic transmutation is a mental art".
>
> *The Kybalion.*

As we have previously mentioned, the Hermetists were the true pioneers of alchemy, astrology, and psychology, with Hermes being the founder of these schools of thought. From astrology would emerge modern astronomy, from alchemy would be born chemistry, and from mystical psychology would develop contemporary psychology. However, we should not assume that the ancients lacked knowledge in areas that modern schools consider their exclusive domain.

The inscriptions carved into the stones and monuments of Egypt conclusively demonstrate that the ancients possessed a perfect knowledge of astronomy. Even the construction of the majestic pyramids reveals a close relationship between their designs and their profound understanding of astronomical science. We should also not underestimate their understanding of chemistry, as fragments of ancient writings discovered reveal their deep familiarity with the chemical properties of substances. In summary, their theories about physics have been confirmed and validated by the most recent discoveries of modern science, particularly regarding the nature of matter.

Far from being unaware of the supposed modern psychological discoveries, the ancient Egyptians were aware of all of it, especially in certain aspects that contemporary schools completely ignore. Particularly in the field of "psychic science", which so perplexes today's psychologists, who eventually come to admit that "after all, there might be some truth to it".

It is undeniable that the ancients possessed profound knowledge beyond chemistry, astronomy, and psychology (specifically in its cerebral aspect). This transcendent knowledge encompassed alchemy, known as the art of transmutation, and transcendental psychology, also referred to as mystical psychology. They mastered not only this internal knowledge but also the external one, the only kind acknowledged by modern scientists. Among the numerous aspects and subjects of the secret knowledge of the hermetists, we find what is known as "mental transmutation", which we will discuss in this chapter.

"Transmutation" is a term typically used to denote the ancient art of transmuting metals, particularly turning base metals into gold. The word "transmute" means "to change from one nature, form, or substance into another, to transform" (Merriam Webster). Consequently, "Mental Transmutation" refers to the art of changing and transforming mental states, forms, and conditions into others. Therefore, it can be seen that Mental Transmutation is the "Art of Mental Chemistry", if one prefers the term, a form of practical Mystical Psychology.

However, this concept extends far beyond what appears at first glance. Alchemical transmutation on the mental plane is so powerful in its effects that, if fully understood, it would become one of the most significant studies for humanity. And this is just the beginning. Let's explore why.

The first of the seven Hermetic principles immerses us in the fascinating world of mentalism, which holds that ALL is mind, that the universe is mental. This statement reveals that the true reality underlying all existence is the mind itself, and that the universe itself is a manifestation created by the mind of the ALL. In the upcoming lessons, we will delve deeper into this principle, but for now, let's explore its effects, assuming this principle is true.

If we accept that the universe is of a mental nature, then mental transmutation becomes the art of changing and transforming the conditions of the universe, whether in relation to matter, energy, or the mind itself. In essence, this transmutation translates into the practice of magic, a topic that has been widely discussed by ancient writers in their mystical works, although they provided few practical instructions on the matter. If everything is mental, then possessing the means to transmute mental conditions grants the Master the power to be the guide and controller of both material conditions and the operations we know as mental.

It is undeniable that only the most advanced mental alchemists have achieved the level of power necessary to master the denser physical conditions, such as natural elements, triggering and calming storms, causing or stopping earthquakes, and other physical phenomena of any nature. The existence of these beings, regardless of the occult school they belong to, is not questioned by any esoteric scholar. The best masters assure their students that such individuals exist, based on personal experiences that justify their belief. These masters do not publicly display their powers, preferring instead to remain in solitude to be able to act and work more effectively on the path of realization. We mention their existence here, only to capture your attention to the fact that their powers are purely mental and operate in harmony with the highest mental transmutation, as established by the principle of mentalism of the Kybalion: *"The universe is a mental creation"*.

However, Hermetic students and initiates in the lower grades than that of Master can also act and work freely in the mental plane. They should not underestimate their ability to influence and work with power in this realm.

The so called "psychic phenomena", "mental influence", and "mentalism", among other terms, are in fact manifestations of mental transmutation. Ultimately, they all originate from a single principle, regardless of the name given to them. Those who dedicate themselves to practicing mental transmutation work in that plane, transforming mental conditions and states into others, following more or less effective formulas. The various "treatments", "affirmations", "auto suggestions", and similar approaches proposed by mentalist schools are precisely these formulas, although they are often imperfect and empirical. Compared to the ancient Masters, most of those who practice them are ignorant, as they lack the fundamental knowledge upon which this operation is based.

Not only is it possible to transmute one's own mental states by following Hermetic methods, but it is also possible to do the same with the mentality of others. In fact, we all experience mental transformations of various kinds, usually unconsciously, but sometimes consciously when we understand the laws and principles governing them. Especially when others are unaware of the means to protect themselves. Many students of mentalism know that material conditions are influenced by the minds of others and can be transmuted and changed according to the desires of those seeking to modify their life circumstances. This knowledge has become so public nowadays that it is unnecessary to go into detail about it. Our purpose here is simply to show the action of this Hermetic principle underlying all the various forms of operation, whether beneficial or harmful, as the force can be used in both directions, according to the Hermetic principle of polarity.

In this small book, we will expound on the fundamental principles of Mental Transmutation, so that all who read it may understand the Underlying Principles and thus possess the Master Key that will unlock the numerous doors of the Principle of Polarity. We will now proceed to consider the first of the Seven Hermetic Principles: the Principle of Mentalism, which explains the truth that "THE ALL is Mind; the Universe is Mental", in the words of The Kybalion. We request the detailed attention and careful study of this great Principle by our students, as it is truly the Fundamental Principle of all Hermetic Philosophy and the Hermetic Art of Mental Transmutation.

CHAPTER IV

"Beneath, and behind, the Universe, Time, Space, and everything that moves and changes, there always lies the Substantial Reality, the Fundamental Truth".

The Kybalion

"Substance" means: "that which underlies all outward manifestations; the essence; the essential reality; the thing in itself", etc. "Substantial" means: "to really exist; to be the essential element; to be real", etc. "Reality" means: "the state of being real; true; lasting; valid; fixed; permanent; actual", etc.

Beyond appearances and external manifestations, there always exists a substantial reality. This is an undeniable law. When a human being contemplates and examines the universe, of which they are a part, they perceive constant change in matter, forces, and mental states. They observe that nothing is truly static; everything transforms and modifies. Nothing endures: every thing is born, grows, dies. At the moment something reaches its maximum development, its decline begins. The law of rhythm is always in action; there are no certainties, nothing is solid, lasting, or substantial, nothing is permanent, everything is in constant change. All things arise and evolve from other things. There is continuous action followed by its corresponding reaction. Everything flows and ebbs, everything is built and falls apart, everything is creation and destruction, life and death. If the human being, upon examining all this, is a thoughtful thinker, they will understand that all these perpetual changes can only be simple external appearances or manifestations of some hidden power behind them, of some substantial reality enclosed in its essence.

All thinkers, regardless of their origin or era, have had to affirm the existence of this essential reality. All philosophical currents, regardless of their denomination, have been based on this notion. To this essential reality, men have given various names: some have called it "God", others have named it "Infinite Divinity" or "Eternal Energy", "Matter", among others, but all have recognized its existence. Its evidence is undeniable in itself, it does not require arguments.

In these lessons, we have followed the example of the most prominent thinkers of all ages, both ancient and modern, the Hermetic Masters, and have named that force hidden behind all manifestations, that essential reality, with the Hermetic term "THE ALL". We believe this term is the broadest that a human being can use.

We accept and share the theories of the great Hermetic thinkers, as well as the ideas of those enlightened souls who have reached higher planes of existence. Both groups affirm that the essential nature of THE ALL is incomprehensible. And this is, undoubtedly, true, as no one, except THE ALL itself, can understand its own essence and existence. The Hermetists believe and teach that THE ALL in itself is and must be unknowable. They consider the theories and speculations of theologians and metaphysicians about the inner nature of THE ALL as mere childish attempts of mortal minds to uncover the secret of the Infinite. All these efforts have always failed and will continue to fail due to the nature of the endeavor itself. Those who venture into such speculations find themselves trapped in a labyrinth of thought with no way out, and if they persist in their attempt, they end up losing all capacity for sane reasoning, until life itself becomes impossible for them. They would be in a situation akin to a squirrel trapped in a cage, spinning endlessly on its wheel, making no progress and remaining as imprisoned as at the beginning.

And even more presumptuous are those who attempt to ascribe to THE ALL the personality, qualities, properties, characteristics, and attributes of themselves, as if THE ALL could experience the emotions, feelings, and human characteristics. They even go so far as to assign it negative qualities, such as jealousy, susceptibility to flattery and prayer, the desire to be venerated and worshiped, and all those things that have been bequeathed to us from the earliest days of humanity's infancy. Such ideas hold no value for those who have evolved and end up discarding them completely.

We believe it is important to make a distinction between philosophy and metaphysics. To us, religion involves the intuitive realization of the existence of THE ALL and the relationship between oneself and IT, while theology refers to human efforts to attribute their own qualities, personality, characteristics, etc., as well as their theories, projects, desires, and designs, assuming the role of intermediary between THE ALL and the people. Philosophy, on the other hand, focuses on speculation seeking to understand things that are cognizable and thinkable (allow us the use of the word), while metaphysics ventures into attempting to explore the nebulous regions of the incognizable and unthinkable, which ultimately shares the same tendency as theology. Therefore, religion and philosophy represent realities in themselves, while theology and metaphysics are like tortuous and labyrinthine paths in which ignorance moves, forming the most insecure and unstable foundation on which the human mind or soul can lean. We will not insist that these definitions be accepted; we mention them only for the purpose of outlining our position. In any case, we will speak very little about theology and metaphysics in these lessons.

While it's true that the very essence of THE ALL is incomprehensible, there are certain truths linked to its existence that the human mind is compelled to accept. The analysis of these truths appears as a suitable topic for investigation, particularly concerning the impressions that the enlightened transmit to us from the higher planes of existence. And it is precisely to this investigation that we invite you at this moment.

> *"What constitutes the fundamental Truth, the substantial Reality, is beyond any denomination, but the wise call it THE ALL".* The Kybalion.
>
> *"In its essence, THE ALL is unknowable".* The Kybalion.
>
> *"But the verdict of reason must be received hospitably, and treated with respect".* The Kybalion.

Human reason, whose judgment we must consider as we see fit, tells us regarding THE ALL, without attempting to unravel the veil of the unknowable:

1. THE ALL must be all that truly is. Nothing can exist outside of THE ALL, otherwise, THE ALL would cease to be what it is.

2. THE ALL must be infinite, as there can be nothing to define, limit, or impose restrictions upon THE ALL. It must be infinite in time, eternal in nature, for it has never ceased to exist and will never be created, as something cannot arise from nothing. It has always existed, in a constant continuum. There cannot be a single moment in which it has not been, for it would be impossible for something to emerge from nothing. It must endure forever, for there is nothing that can destroy it, and it can never cease to be, not even for a brief moment, for something cannot turn into nothing.

Moreover, THE ALL must be infinite in space, existing everywhere, for there is nothing and no place beyond its reach. Its presence must be continuous and omnipresent in space, without interruption or separation, as there is nothing within IT that can be interrupted, separated, or broken in its complete continuity. Furthermore, there is nothing that can "fill the voids".

THE ALL must also be infinite in power, absolute in its nature, as nothing can limit, restrict, confine, or obstruct it. It is not subject to any external power, for there is no other power beyond its own.

3. THE ALL must be immutable, meaning it is not subject to change in its real essence, as there is nothing that can compel it to change or that it could have transformed from. It cannot be increased or decreased, nor become larger or smaller in any aspect. It has always existed, and will continue to exist forever, identical to what it is at this moment: THE ALL. There has never been, there is not, nor will there ever be something into which it can transform or change.

Since THE ALL is Infinite, Absolute, Eternal, and Immutable, it follows that anything that is limited, changeable, transformable, and conditioned cannot be THE ALL. And since nothing truly exists outside of IT, anything that is finite must essentially be nothing. Do not worry or be alarmed; we are not leading you toward Christian Science while cloaking these teachings under the name of Hermetic Philosophy. There is a reconciliation between these seemingly contradictory subjects. Be patient, as in time we will address all of this.

When we look around us, we see what we call "matter", which constitutes the physical foundation of all forms. Is THE ALL merely matter? Absolutely not. Matter cannot manifest Life or Mind, and since mind is manifested in the universe, THE ALL cannot be simply matter. Nothing can rise above its own source, nothing can manifest in an effect if it is not also present in the cause, nothing can evolve or emerge as a result if it is not involved or involuted as an antecedent.

Moreover, modern science reveals to us that matter does not truly exist, but is "interrupted energy or force", that is, energy or force at a lower degree of vibration. As a recent writer has stated, "matter is submerged in Mystery". Even materialistic science has abandoned the theory of matter and now relies on the concept of "energy".

Then, is the ALL simply a force or energy? No. Force, as conceived by materialists, is something blind, mechanical, devoid of life or mentality. Life and mind cannot arise from blind energy, for the reasons we have previously mentioned: "Nothing can rise above its own source, nothing evolves if it has not involuted, nothing manifests in an effect if it is not present in the cause". Therefore, the ALL cannot be merely force or energy, because if it were, there would be no such thing as mind and life, and we both know they exist, since we are alive and using our minds to reflect on this matter. Equally are those who claim that energy is everything.

What is there in the Universe beyond matter and energy, and what we know is present? Life and mind in all their various stages of development! Then you might ask: Do you mean that the ALL is life and mind? Our answer is yes and no. If you refer to what we, mere mortals, understand by life and mind: No, the ALL is not that! But what kind of life and mentality do you refer to? you might inquire.

The answer is a living mind, as vast as our capacity to conceive it, as life and mind far surpass mere mechanical force or matter. An infinite and living mind compared to finite life and mentality. We refer to that which enlightened souls attempt to convey when they reverently utter the word: SPIRIT!

The ALL is a living and infinite mind,
the enlightened call it Spirit.

CHAPTER V

THE MENTAL UNIVERSE

"The universe is a mental creation held in the mind of THE ALL".
The Kybalion.

THE ALL is spirit. But what is spirit? That question cannot be answered, as attempting to define it would virtually be defining THE ALL, something that cannot be explained. Spirit is simply the name humans give to the highest conception of the Infinite Living Mind. It represents the real essence, something so superior to what we understand by mind and life as these are to energy and matter. Spirit transcends our understanding, and we use this term in the same sense and with the intention of referring to the same thing as when we talk about THE ALL. For our understanding, we may conceive of spirit as an Infinite Living Mind, though at the same time we recognize that we cannot fully comprehend it. Either we do this, or we are forced to stop thinking.

Now we will proceed to examine the nature of the Universe in its entirety, as well as in its parts. What is the Universe? We have previously affirmed that nothing can exist outside of THE ALL; then, is the Universe THE ALL? No, it cannot be, as the Universe appears to be composed of many individual units and is in constant change. Moreover, it does not align with the ideas we have accepted regarding THE ALL, as we indicated in our previous lesson. Then, if the Universe is not THE ALL, must it be nothing? This is the inevitable conclusion that apparently presents itself in our mind. However, this does not satisfy the question, as we are conscious and perceive the existence of the Universe. If the Universe is something and not THE ALL, what can it be? Let's examine it in detail.

If the Universe undeniably exists, or at least appears to do so, it must arise in some way from THE ALL, being its creation. However, since something cannot arise from nothing, in what manner could THE ALL have originated it? Some philosophers have attempted to answer this question by arguing that THE ALL created the Universe from itself, extracting it from its own substance. Nevertheless, this answer is unsatisfactory, as THE ALL cannot be increased, diminished, or divided, as we have already established. Even if it were possible, each particle of the Universe could not claim to certainly be THE ALL, as it cannot lose the knowledge of itself nor transform into an atom, a blind force, or a lower living being.

Some individuals, upon understanding that THE ALL encompasses everything and recognizing their own existence, have reached an extraordinary conclusion: they and THE ALL are identical. Brandishing their claim of "I am God" with pride, they have delighted the masses and elicited pity from the wises.

If an atom dared to exclaim with determination "I am human", even then it would be considered modest in comparison.

But, what is the Universe if it is not THE ALL and has not been created by being separated from its own essence? What else could it be? Or better yet, how else could it have been conceived? This is the great question that we pose to ourselves. Fortunately, the principle of correspondence (as set forth in chapter I) comes to our aid. The ancient Hermetic axiom "as above, so below" can now be employed to shed light on this point. Let us attempt, therefore, to understand something of what happens on higher planes by examining what occurs on our own plane. The principle of correspondence can be applied here, just as it can to any other dilemma. Let's see:

In their own plane of existence, how does a human being create? Firstly, they can create by building or fabricating something using the materials the external world provides. However, this idea does not help us, as outside of THE ALL there are no materials with which it could create. Secondly, human beings can create through fertilization, which is nothing more than their ability to multiply accompanied by the transfer of a part of their own essence into the womb of the mother. However, this possibility also does not serve us, as THE ALL cannot transfer or subtract a portion of itself, nor can it reproduce or multiply. In the first case, it would imply a subtraction or addition from its own essence to THE ALL, which is absurd.

Is there no other means by which man creates? Yes, there is another: mental creation. In creating in this manner, he does not use materials provided by the external world, nor does he reproduce himself, and yet, his spirit permeates his mental creation.

Following the principle of correspondence, it can be justifiably thought that the ALL creates the Universe mentally, in a way similar to the process by which man creates his mental images. And here in this description coincide both the judgment given by reason and that of the enlightened souls, as can be found in their writings or teachings. Such are the doctrines of the wise. Such are those taught by Hermes.

The ALL cannot create in any way except mentally, without using materials (for there are none), nor reproducing (which is also impossible). There is no escape from this conclusion of reason, which, as we have already seen, agrees perfectly with what the enlightened say. Just as you can create a universe in your own mind, so the ALL creates the Kosmos in its own.

Does the human being have no other way of creating? Yes, there is another: mental creation. In creating in this way, one does not use materials from the external world nor reproduce oneself; yet, one's spirit permeates one's mental creation.

Following the principle of correspondence, it is reasonable to think that the ALL creates the Universe in a mental manner, similar to the process through which a human being brings to life their mental images. It is remarkable how this description coincides both with the conclusion reached by reason and with the teachings of the enlightened souls, as can be found in their writings and discourses. These are the doctrines of the wise, the teachings transmitted by Hermes.

The ALL cannot create in any other way except through the mind, without using materials (since none exist), nor reproducing (which is also impossible). There is no escape from this logical conclusion, which, as we have seen, aligns perfectly with what is expressed by the enlightened. Just as you can create a universe in your own mind, in the same way, the ALL brings the Kosmos to life in its own essence.

However, the universe established by you would be the creation of a limited mind, whereas the ALL would give rise to an infinite creation. Both are similar in nature but differ greatly in their scope. As we progress in our study, we will explore in greater detail the process of creation and manifestation. But for now, you must anchor in your minds this fundamental point: the Universe and everything it contains is a mental creation of the ALL; everything is mind.

> "The ALL gives life in its infinite mind to countless universes, which exist over eons of time, and yet, to It, the creation, development, decay, and death of a million universes are but the twinkling of an instant".
>
> *The Kybalion.*

The principle of gender, present in all planes of life (as explained in Chapter I and others to come), manifests in the material, mental, and spiritual realms. However, as we have previously mentioned, "gender" does not merely refer to "sex", which is just the physical expression of gender. "Gender" encompasses everything related to generation or creation. And wherever something is generated or created, regardless of the plane on which it occurs, the principle of gender is present. This holds true even in the creation of universes.

Now, do not misinterpret our words as suggesting the existence of a masculine and a feminine creator god. That would simply be a misrepresentation of the ancient teachings on the subject. The truth is that the ALL, in its essence, transcends gender, just as it transcends all other laws, including those of time and space. It is the law from which all laws emanate, and therefore cannot be subject to them. However, when the ALL manifests on the plane of generation or creation, it acts in accordance with the laws and the Principle, as it is operating at a lower level of existence. Consequently, the principle of gender manifests, both in its masculine and feminine aspects, on the mental plane, of course.

This idea may seem startling when first heard, though on other occasions you have passively accepted it in your everyday conceptions. You speak of the fatherhood of God and the motherhood of Nature, of God as a divine father and Nature as a Universal mother. In this way, you have instinctively perceived the principle of Gender in the Universe, have you not?

However, the Hermetic teachings do not imply a real duality, for the ALL is ONE, and the two aspects are merely phases of manifestation. The doctrine maintains that the masculine principle, manifested by the ALL, remains in some manner apart from the mental creation of the Universe. It projects its will upon the feminine principle (which can be termed nature), and it is at this point that the evolutionary work of a Universe begins, from simple "centers of activity" to human beings and even higher planes of existence, all according to well established laws of Nature. If you prefer the ancient mental representations, you may conceive of the masculine principle as God, the father, and the feminine principle as Nature, the universal mother, from whose womb all things are born. This goes beyond a mere poetic figure; it is an idea about the process of creation of a Universe. Yet, always remember that the ALL is ONE, and it is within its infinite mind that the Kosmos are created, generated, and exist.

It might help you to properly conceive this if you apply the principle of correspondence in your own mind. You know that part of you that you call "I", in a certain way, stays apart from the creation and mental images in your intellect. The part of the mind where images are generated may be called the "me", in contrast to the "I", which remains apart and examines the thoughts, ideas, and images of the "me". As "as above, so below", remember, the phenomena of one plane can be used to solve the enigmas of higher and lower planes.

Is it not amazing that you, as children, feel a deep respect for Father Mother? Is it not wonderful that when you consider the works and wonders of Nature, you are moved to the depths of your being? It is to your mind mother that you draw near, as a child snuggles in the lap of its mother.

Do not suppose that the tiny world around you, the Earth, which is but a grain of sand in the vast Universe, is the universe itself. There are millions and millions of such worlds, some even larger than ours. And there are millions upon millions of universes that exist in the Mind of the One. Even within our solar system, there exist realms and planes of life much higher than ours, and beings comparable to us as amoebas are to man. There are beings whose powers and attributes far exceed those of humans, something that man has not even dreamed could exist. However, despite this, these beings were once what we are now, and we will one day be what they are, and even more, for such is the destiny of man, as revealed to us by the enlightened.

Death holds no true reality, not even in a relative sense: it is simply a rebirth into new life, ascending to ever higher planes of existence over eons and eons of time. The universe is our home, our dwelling, and we can explore it to its farthest reaches before the consummation of time. We reside in the mind of the ALL, and our possibilities and opportunities are infinite, both in time and space. And at the end of the great cycle of eons, when the ALL draws its creations back into itself, we shall march joyfully, for then we shall be able to fully comprehend the truth of being ONE with the ALL. So assure us the enlightened ones, those who have made significant progress on the path of realization.

Meanwhile, let us remain calm and serene; we are safe and protected by the Infinite Power of the Father Mother Mind.

"In the Mind of the Father-Mother, the children are at home".

The Kybalion

"There is no one who does not have a father and mother in the Universe".

CHAPTER VI

THE DIVINE PARADOX

"The half-wise, recognizing the relative unreality of the Universe, imagine that they may defy its laws. But in truth, they are but vain and presumptuous fools bound to be dashed against the rocks and torn asunder by the elements due to their folly. On the other hand, the truly wise, understanding the nature of the Universe, use the Law against the laws: the higher against the lower. Through alchemy, they transmute the undesirable into something valuable, thus triumphing. Mastery lies not in abnormal dreams, visions, or phantasmal images, but in the wise use of higher forces against the lower, vibrating on the higher frequencies. Transmutation, not presumptuous denial, is the Master's weapon".

The Kybalion

This is the paradox of the Universe, arising from the principle of polarity, which manifests when the ALL begins to create

Though for the infinite ALL, the Universe with its laws, powers, life, and phenomena might seem like mere visions in a state of meditation or dream, the Universe must be treated as real. Life, actions, and thoughts should be grounded in it, in accordance with this reality, even though each one possesses a clear knowledge and understanding of the Higher Truth in relation to their own plane and laws. If the ALL had conceived the Universe as something real, it would be catastrophic, for there would be no possibility to ascend from the lower to the higher. The universe would have become a fixed and immovable entity, and progress would become impossible. And if a human, with their half wisdom, acts, lives, and thinks in the Universe as if it were a dream, akin to their own limited dreams, then so it will be for them. Like a walking corpse, they will find themselves going in circles without advancing, until they are finally forced to wake up and live according to the natural laws they have forgotten. Always keep our minds focused on the Star, but take care where we place our feet lest we fall into an abyss. Always remember the divine paradox that states, "though the Universe is not, yet it is". Always keep in mind the two poles of truth: the absolute and the relative. Avoid half truths.

What the Hermetists call the "Law of Paradox" is an aspect of the principle of polarity. The Hermetic teachings are filled with references to this paradox that reveals itself in every aspect of life and being. The masters always strive to prevent their students from overlooking the "other side" of any matter, and their recommendations are particularly focused on issues related to the absolute and the relative, which often confuse students of philosophy and lead them to act and think contrary to what is considered "common sense". We urge our students to thoroughly understand the divine paradox between the absolute and the relative, avoiding being hypnotized by the false illusion of half truths. This lesson has been written from this perspective. Read it carefully.

The first idea that comes to mind for the thinker who has understood and realized the truth that the Universe is a mental creation of the ALL, is that the Universe and all it contains are mere illusion, unreality. However, this idea is immediately met with an internal revolution. But like other great truths, this must be considered from both absolute and relative viewpoints. Of course, in comparison to the ALL itself, the Universe is an illusion, a dream, a fantasy. We recognize this when we speak of the world as a fleeting dream, born and dying. Everything that is mutable, changing, finite, and insubstantial is linked to the notion of a created Universe when compared to the ALL itself, regardless of our belief about the nature of both.

Philosophers, metaphysicians, scientists, and theologians all agree on this, and this conception is found in all philosophical and religious systems, as well as in the respective theories of metaphysical and theological schools.

The Hermetic teachings do not proclaim the insubstantiality of the Universe more emphatically than what you're accustomed to, although the presentation of the subject might seem some what more forceful to you. Anything that has a beginning and an end, in a certain sense, must be unreal and illusory, and the Universe is in this situation, regardless of the thought system to which you belong. From an absolute perspective, there is only one reality, the ALL, no matter the terms we use to reflect or debate on it. Whether the Universe was created from matter or is a mental creation in the mind of the ALL, it is insubstantial, changing, subject to time, space, and change. We must understand and assimilate this before reflecting and examining the Hermetic conception of the mental nature of the Universe. Examine any other conception and see if any of them denies this.

However, the absolute perspective only reveals one aspect of the matter, the other side is the relative aspect. Absolute truths have been defined as "things as the mind of God knows and sees them", while relative truths are "things as the highest reason of the human being comprehends them". Thus, while for the ALL the Universe may be illusory and unreal, a mere dream or product of meditation, to the limited minds that are part of that Universe and observe through their mortal faculties, the Universe is certainly real and must be regarded as such. By recognizing this absolute perspective, we do not make the mistake of ignoring or denying the facts and phenomena of the Universe as they present themselves to our mortal faculties: we are not the ALL, let's remember that.

To put it in more familiar terms, we can acknowledge the fact that matter "exists" to our senses, and it would be a serious mistake if we did not admit it. However, our limited mind recognizes the scientific truth that there is no such thing as matter from the point of view of science, and that what we call matter is nothing more than a collection of atoms, which in turn are units of force grouped that we call "electrons" or "ions", which constantly vibrate in circular motions. We strike a stone and feel the impact, it seems real, but we know it is nothing more than what has already been explained.

But let us remember that our foot, which feels the impact through the intervention of the brain, is composed of the same matter, of electrons, just like our brain. And, ultimately, if it were not for the mind, we would know absolutely nothing about either the foot or the stone.

Furthermore, the ideal that an artist or sculptor tries to capture in marble or on canvas seems extremely real to them. The same is true for the characters created in the mind of a playwright, who seeks to express them so that others may recognize them. And if this is true for our limited minds, what would be the degree of reality of the mental images generated in the mind of the Infinite? Oh, for us mortals, this universe of mentality is truly tangible! It is the only thing we will ever know, even as we ascend from plane to plane, ever higher. To know it in any other way, through actual experience, we would have to be the ALL itself. It is undeniable that the higher we ascend on the scale, the closer we come to the mind of the Father and the illusory nature of finite things becomes more apparent. However, it won't be until the ALL completely absorbs us within Itself that this vision will disappear.

Therefore, we need not be deluded by this illusion. Instead, let us recognize the true nature of the Universe and strive to understand its mental laws, applying them most effectively for our upward progress through life, as we journey from one plane of being to another. The laws of the Universe remain "laws of iron" even if they are of a mental nature. All, except the ALL, are subject to them. What resides in the infinite mind of the ALL is real, just one degree below the very reality that constitutes the nature of the ALL.

We need not feel insecure or fearful; we should perceive ourselves as firmly sustained in the infinite mind, where nothing can harm or instill fear in us. Outside of the ALL, there is no power that can affect us. We can remain calm and secure. And in this realization, once achieved, lies a fullness of security and serenity. Then, we will sleep in peace upon the incomprehensible solidity of the Deep and rest confidently upon the Ocean of the Infinite Mind that encompasses the ALL. In Him, without a doubt, we live, move, and exist.

Matter does not lose its nature of a solid structure for us while we remain in this plane, even though we know it is nothing more than a clustering of particles of force, called electrons, which vibrate rapidly and revolve around each other forming atoms. These atoms, in turn, spin and vibrate to constitute molecules, and the combination of these molecules forms the large masses of matter. And it will be no less matter simply because, as we advance in our research, we discover that the force, whose units are electrons, are nothing but manifestations of the mind of the ALL, and that, like everything in the universe, its nature is purely mental. Although on the plane of Matter we must recognize its phenomena, we can master it (as all masters do to a greater or lesser extent) by applying higher forces upon it. It would be an act of madness to deny the existence of matter in this relative aspect. We can, indeed, deny its dominion over us; that is fine, but we must not attempt to ignore it in its relative aspect, at least while we live in this plane.

Matter does not lose its nature of a solid structure for us while we remain in this plane, even though we know it is nothing more than a clustering of particles of force, called electrons, which vibrate rapidly and revolve around each other forming atoms. These atoms, in turn, spin and vibrate to constitute molecules, and the combination of these molecules forms the large masses of matter. And it will be no less matter simply because, as we advance in our research, we discover that the force, whose units are electrons, are nothing but manifestations of the mind of the ALL, and that, like everything in the universe, its nature is purely mental. Although on the plane of Matter we must recognize its phenomena, we can master it (as all masters do to a greater or lesser extent) by applying higher forces upon it. It would be an act of madness to deny the existence of matter in this relative aspect. We can, indeed, deny its dominion over us; that is fine, but we must not attempt to ignore it in its relative aspect, at least while we live in this plane.

The Hermetic Principle of Mentalism, explaining the true nature of the Universe as being fundamentally mental, does not contradict scientific conceptions about the Universe, life, or evolution. In fact, science only corroborates Hermetic teachings. These teachings assert that the nature of the Universe is mental, while science holds that it is "material"; or according to the latest views, ultimately "energy". The Hermetic teachings also do not conflict with the fundamental principle of Herbert Spencer[11], who posited the

11 Herbert Spencer was an English philosopher, sociologist, and evolutionary theorist, born on April 27, 1820, and died on December 8, 1903. He is recognized for his contribution to the development of evolutionary theory, as well as his influence in fields such as sociology, psychology, and ethics.

Spencer is primarily known for his concept of "social Darwinism", which applied Charles Darwin's principles of natural selection to the development of human societies. He argued that societies evolved from simple to complex forms, and that those individuals and groups best adapted survived and thrived while the less fit lagged behind.

existence of an "Infinite and Eternal Energy from which all things emanate". Indeed, Hermetists regard Spencer's philosophy as the highest expression of the working of natural laws ever promulgated. They believe that Spencer was the reincarnation of an ancient philosopher who lived in Egypt thousands of years ago and later as Heraclitus, the Greek philosopher of 500 B.C. They consider his doctrine of "infinite and eternal energy" to be in line with Hermetic teachings, with the addition that this energy is the mind of the ALL. With this master key of Hermetic philosophy, Spencer's student can unlock many doors of the internal philosophical conceptions of the great English philosopher, whose works demonstrate the results of his preparation in his previous incarnations. His teachings on Evolution and Rhythm are in almost perfect harmony with the Hermetic Doctrine of the Principle of Rhythm.

Therefore, the student does not need to discard scientific viewpoints about the Universe. All that is asked of them is to understand the fundamental principle that ALL is mind, that the Universe is mental: firmly hold this in the mind of ALL. And they will discover that the other six principles perfectly align with this scientific knowledge and will serve to clarify the obscure points. This should not surprise us when we consider the influence that Hermetic thought had on the early philosophers of Greece, whose doctrines largely form the basis of current scientific theories. The

---

In addition to his work in sociology, Spencer also formulated theories in areas such as psychology, ethics, and epistemology. His most notable work is "A System of Synthetic Philosophy", a series of books in which he developed a unified view of reality, integrating biological and social evolution into a coherent philosophical framework.

Throughout his life, Herbert Spencer generated extensive intellectual debate, and his influence extended both in his time and in subsequent generations. His ideas and theories have left a lasting mark on the history of scientific and philosophical thought

acceptance of the first Hermetic principle (Mentalism) is the only significant difference between modern science and Hermetic students, and science is gradually moving towards that point as it progresses through the darkness and finds its way in the labyrinth it has entered in search of Reality.

The purpose of this lesson is to impress upon the student's mind the fact that the Universe, its laws, and phenomena are equally real, as far as human beings are concerned, whether under the hypothesis of materialism or energy. Under either hypothesis, the Universe, in its external aspect, is always changing and transient, therefore lacking substantial reality. However, it must be noted that the other pole of truth exists: under either of these hypotheses, we are compelled to act and live as if those ephemeral things were real and substantial. The difference lies in the fact that the power of the mind was previously unknown as a Natural Force, whereas now we see that Mentalism is the most powerful force of its kind. This single difference is sufficient to revolutionize the lives of those who understand the principle, practice, and resulting laws.

Once the advantage of Mentalism is understood, one learns to know, use, and apply the resulting laws. However, one must not fall into the temptation that, as The Kybalion indicates, lurks for those half wise individuals who become hypnotized by the apparent unreality of things, whose consciousness wanders as if in a dream, living in a world of fantasy and unaware of everyday life and work; their destiny is to crash against the rocks and dissolve into the elements due to their madness. Instead, let us follow the example of the sage that the same authority points to: "To use the Law against the laws; the superior against the inferior, and through the art of alchemy transmute the undesirable into valuable, triumphing in that way". According to this doctrine, we must avoid half wisdom, which is madness and ignores the truth that: "Mastery does not reside in abnormal dreams, visions, or fantastic imaginations, but in using superior forces against the inferior, thus escaping the suffering of the lower planes by rising to the higher ones". Always remember that "transmutation and not presumptuous denial is the weapon of the Master". These quoted passages belong to The Kybalion, and it is important to keep them in mind at all times.

We do not dwell in a world of dreams, but in a Universe that, though relative, is real, at least insofar as our life and actions are concerned. Our mission in this Universe is not to deny its existence but to live, using its laws appropriately to ascend from the inferior to the superior, living and acting to the best of our ability within the circumstances that arise day by day, and striving, as much as possible, to manifest our highest ideas and ideals. The true meaning of life is not known to man on this plane, if anyone knows it at all, but the wisest, and our own intuitions as well, teach us that we will not go wrong if we strive to live in the best possible way and follow the universal trend in the same direction, despite apparent evidence to the contrary. We are all on the Path, and this path always rises, with frequent resting places.

Let us heed the message of The Kybalion and follow the example of the sage, avoiding the error of the half wise, who perish due to their madness.

CHAPTER VII

"THE ALL" IN ALL

"While it is true that everything exists within the ALL, it is equally true that the ALL is found in all things. One who comprehends this properly has gained great knowledge".

The Kybalion.

How many times have we heard the majority repeat the assertion that their Deity was "all in all", and how little we have suspected the profound hidden meaning behind those words spoken without reflection. The commonly used expression is what has survived from the hermetic maxim of the epigraph. As The Kybalion tells us: "One who comprehends it properly has attained great knowledge". If this is true, let us try to understand what it really means, given its immense importance.

Within that maxim lies one of the greatest philosophical, scientific, and religious truths.

We have already imparted the Hermetic teaching regarding the mental nature of the Universe, the truth that "the Universe is Mental, held in the mind of the ALL". As The Kybalion states in the cited passage: "all things are in the ALL". However, we must also note the following correlated statement: “It is equally true that the ALL is in all things”. This apparent contradiction can be reconciled through the law of Paradox. Furthermore, it is a precise Hermetic statement about the relationships that exist within the ALL and its mental Universe. We have already seen how everything is contained in the ALL; now let us examine the second aspect of the matter.

The Hermetic doctrine maintains that the ALL is imminent and inherent in the Universe, present everywhere, in every particle, unit, or combination within it.

Masters often illustrate this postulate through the Principle of Correspondence. The instructor asks the student to form a mental image of something, whether it be a person, an idea, or any other thing with a mental form. The preferred example is usually that of an author creating an idea of characters or that of a painter or sculptor shaping the mental image of what they seek to express through their art. In each case, the student will observe that even though the image has existence and exists only within their own mind, they themselves, as a thinker, author, painter, or sculptor, are, in a certain sense, immanent in that image. In other words, all the virtue, life, spirit, or reality of the mental image is derived from the “immanent mind” of the thinker. Let us reflect on this for a moment until we fully grasp the idea.

Taking another example, we could say that Othello, Iago, Hamlet, Lear, Richard III, and so on, existed in Shakespeare’s mind at the moment of their conception or creation. And yet, Shakespeare also existed within each of those characters, imparting to them their vitality, their spirit, and their action.

What is the spirit of the characters we know as Micawber, Oliver Twist, Uriah Heep?... Is it Charles Dickens, or do each of them possess a personal spirit, independent of their creator? Do the Venus de Medici, the Sistine Madonna, the Apollo Belvedere have their own spirits and reality, or do they represent the mental and spiritual powers of their creators? The Law of Paradox explains that both propositions are true, depending on the appropriate viewpoints. Micawber is, at the same time, Micawber and Dickens. And while it can be said that Micawber is Dickens, Dickens is not identical to Micawber. Man, as Micawber, can exclaim: "The spirit of my creator is inherent in me, and yet, I am not He". This greatly differs from the deceptive half truth that some pseudo sages proclaim far and wide, saying: "I am God". Imagine poor Micawber or cunning Uriah Heep exclaiming: "I am Dickens", or any other character from Shakespeare's works proclaiming: "I am Shakespeare". The ALL is in the worm, but the worm is far from being the ALL. Although the worm exists merely as a tiny creature, created and having its existence only in the mind of the ALL, the ALL is immanent in it, just as in the particles that make it up. Is there any greater mystery contained in that proposition: "All is in the ALL, and the ALL is in all"?

The student will understand, of course, that the examples mentioned above are inevitably imperfect and insufficient since they represent the creation of mental images in finite minds, while the Universe is the creation of an infinite mind, and the difference between the two poles separates them. However, it is simply a matter of degree, as the same Principle is in operation: the Principle of Correspondence is manifested in each case: "As above, so below; as below, so above".

And as the human being becomes aware of the existence of the Underlying Spirit, immanent within their own being, they will ascend the scale of life. That is what spiritual development implies: the recognition, understanding, and manifestation of the inner Spirit. Let us always remember this definition of spiritual development, for it holds the truth of every genuine Religion.

There are multiple Planes of Being, numerous subplanes of life, various levels of existence in the Universe. And all of them depend on the progress of beings on the scale, where the lowest point is the densest matter, while the highest Being is separated from the Spirit of the ALL only by a subtle division. Throughout this scale of life, everything is in constant motion. All are on the path, whose destination and goal is the ALL. All progress is a return home. Everything rises, advances, despite apparent contradictions. That is the message of the enlightened one.

The Hermetic doctrine regarding the process of the mental creation of the Universe maintains that at the beginning of the creative cycle, the ALL, in its aspect of being, directs its will toward its aspect of "Becoming", and thus begins the process of creation. It is said that this process involves a gradual decrease in vibratory intensity until it reaches a very low level of vibrating energy, at which point the densest form of matter becomes manifest. This process is called involution because the ALL "wraps itself up" in its own creation. This finds its correspondence in the mental processes of an artist, writer, or inventor, who becomes so immersed in their mental creation that they almost completely forget their own existence, for in those moments, they "live in their creation". Perhaps, if instead of using the word "wrapped up", we used the word "absorbed", we could obtain a clearer idea of the intended meaning.

This involutive state of creation is also often referred to as the "Emanation" of divine energy, while the evolutionary state is called "Absorption". The farthest pole of the creative process is considered the most distant from the ALL, while the beginning of the evolutionary state is seen as a swing of the Rhythm pendulum, as a return home.

The teaching tells us that during the Effusion, vibrations gradually dampen until the damping impulse finally ceases, and it is then that the return of the pendulum oscillation occurs. However, there is a difference: while in the effusion, the creative forces manifest compactly as a whole, from the very beginning of the evolutionary state or "reabsorption", the law of individualization manifests, meaning the tendency to separate into units of force. Thus, what left the ALL as undifferentiated energy returns to its original source as countless highly developed units of life, which have ascended further and further up the scale through physical, mental, and spiritual evolution.

The ancient Hermetics used the word "meditation" to describe the process of the mental creation of the Universe in the mind of the ALL, and the word "contemplation" was also frequently employed.

However, the idea they seem to suggest is that of using Divine Attention. "Attention" is a word derived from Latin, meaning "to reach, to arrive", and the act of attention is truly an "extension, a reaching out" of mental energy. Therefore, we will fully understand the concept by examining the true meaning of attention.

The Hermetic doctrine regarding evolution is that the ALL, after meditating on the principle of creation and thus establishing the material foundations of the Cosmos, gradually awakens from its meditation and, in doing so, gives rise to the manifestation of the evolutionary process on the material, mental, and spiritual planes, successively and in order. Thus, the upward movement begins, and all beings are directed towards the Spirit. Matter becomes less dense, units emerge, combinations begin, life appears and manifests in increasingly higher forms, and the mind becomes more evident, vibrating everything with greater intensity. In short, the entire process of evolution, in all its phases, begins and proceeds in accordance with the laws of the "absorption" process. All of this spans eons and eons of time, where each eon is composed of millions of years. However, as the enlightened ones claim, the entire creation, including the involution and evolution of a universe, is but a blink of an eye for the ALL. At the end of countless cycles of eons of time, the ALL withdraws its attention (contemplation) or meditation from the Universe, because the Great Work has been completed, and everything is once again absorbed by the One from which it once emerged.

But the deepest mystery of all is that the Spirit of every soul is not annihilated but expands infinitely, merging the Creator and the Created. That is the voice of enlightenment.

The illumination presented regarding meditation and the subsequent awakening of the ALL is, of course, simply an attempt to describe an infinite process through a finite example. But, nevertheless, "as above, so below". The difference lies only in the degree. Just as the ALL awakens from its meditation on the Universe, in the same way, the human being (in due time) will cease to manifest on the material plane and will withdraw more and more towards their inner spirit, which truly is the "Divine Ego".

There is another topic we wish to discuss in this lesson, delving into the metaphysical realm of speculation, although our purpose is simply to demonstrate the futility of such speculation. We refer to the question that inevitably arises in the minds of all thinkers who have ventured into the search for Truth: Why did the ALL create the Universe? This question can be phrased in different ways, but its essence is always the same.

Humans have struggled greatly to find an answer, but a worthy one has not yet been found. Some have imagined that the ALL would gain something from it, but that is absurd; what could the ALL gain that it does not already possess? Others say that the ALL wishes to love something, or that it created it for its own amusement, or because it felt lonely, or to manifest its power. However, all these answers are childish and puerile, belonging to the early childhood of thought.

Some have tried to explain the mystery by presuming that the ALL was "compelled" to create due to its "inner nature" or its "creative instinct".

While this idea represents an advancement over the others, it has a weak point. If its "inner nature" or "creative instinct" compelled it to act, then that inner nature or creative instinct would be the

Absolute rather than the ALL, and thus the proposition fails at its very foundation. However, the ALL does create and manifest, and it seems to find a certain satisfaction in doing so. It is very difficult to escape the conclusion that to some infinite degree, there must be something corresponding to an inner nature or creative instinct in the human being, with a corresponding infinite desire and will. It could not act if it did not desire it, it could not do it unless it wanted to, and it would not want it if it did not find satisfaction in it. All these things would belong to an inner nature, and its existence could be postulated according to the Law of Correspondence, both internal and external. This is the problem found at the root of the difficulty, and the difficulty found at the very root of the problem.

Strictly speaking, it cannot be said that there is a "reason" to act because a reason implies a cause, and the ALL is beyond cause and effect, except when its own will becomes a cause, at which point the principle is set in motion. Therefore, one cannot reason about the matter itself because the ALL is unknowable. Just as we are compelled to say simply: THE ALL IS, we can only say that THE ALL ACTS BECAUSE IT ACTS. And ultimately, the ALL is the reason in itself, and it can truly be stated that It is its own reason, its own law, its own act, or better yet: that the ALL, its reason, its act, and its law are one, with the different words being different names for the same thing. In the view of those writing this, the answer is found enclosed in the inner being of the ALL, in its secret being. The Law of Correspondence, in our view, only reaches the aspect of the ALL that we call the aspect of becoming or state. Behind that aspect is the aspect of being, in which all laws dissolve into the Law, all principles into the Principle, and the ALL, the Principle, and Being are identical, one and the same.

Therefore, any metaphysical speculation on this point is futile. If we address this issue here, it is only to demonstrate that while we acknowledge the fact, we also recognize the absurdity of the answers given by metaphysicians and theologians.

In conclusion, it may be interesting for students to know that while some of the ancient and modern hermetic instructors tend to apply the Principle of Correspondence to this question, leading to the notion of an "inner nature", it is said that Hermes the Great, when asked this question by some of his more advanced students, simply pressed his lips tightly and did not utter a word, as if to indicate that there was no answer. Perhaps he wished to apply the axiom of this philosophy that states "the lips of Wisdom are closed, except to the ears of understanding", believing that even his most accomplished disciples did not possess the necessary understanding to be taught such knowledge. In any case, if Hermes possessed the Secret, he did not share it, and at least as far as the world is concerned, the lips of Hermes remain sealed on the matter. And if Hermes the Great hesitated to speak, who would be the bold mortal to attempt to teach it?

But let us remember that, whatever the answer to this problem, if there is one, the truth remains: "While it is true that everything is in the ALL, it is no less true that the ALL is in all things". The statement at this point is emphatic. And to conclude, we will repeat the words of the quote: "He who properly understands this has acquired great knowledge".

CHAPTER VIII

THE PLANES OF CORRESPONDENCE

"As above, so below; as below, so above".
The Kybalion.

The second great Hermetic principle embodies the truth that there is harmony, agreement, and correspondence between the various planes of manifestation, life, and being. This truth holds because everything in the Universe originates from the same source, and the same laws, principles, and characteristics apply to each unit or combination of units of activity, as each manifests its own phenomena on its own plane.

To facilitate meditation and study, Hermetic Philosophy considers that the Universe can be divided into three major classes of phenomena, known as the Three Great Planes:

I. The Physical Plane.

II. The Mental Plane.

III. The Spiritual Plane.

These divisions are more or less artificial and arbitrary, for in reality, the three divisions are simply ascending degrees on the great scale of life. The lowest point corresponds to undifferentiated matter, while the highest is that of Spirit. Furthermore, the different planes interpenetrate one another, so a clear and distinct division cannot be established between the uppermost part of the Physical Plane and the lower part of the Mental Plane.

In short, the three great planes can be regarded as three major groups of degrees of life in manifestation. Although the purpose of this book does not allow us to delve into a comprehensive explanation of them, we will provide a general description.

To begin with, we can consider the question often posed by beginners who wish to understand what the word "Plane" really means, a term that is freely used but rarely explained in occult works. The question is often framed as follows: "Is a Plane a place with dimensions, or is it simply a condition or state?" And we can answer: "No, it is not a place or an ordinary dimension of space; however, it is more than a state or condition". It can be considered a state or condition, but even so, the state or condition is a dimensional degree, a scale that is subject to measurement. This may seem like a paradox, but let's examine the point. A "dimension" is a straight line measurement related to a base measurement, etc. The ordinary dimensions of space are height, width, and depth. But there is another dimension of created things, another straight line measurement, known to occultists and also to scientists, although the latter have not yet given it the name of dimension. This new dimension, which is currently the basis for much speculation under the name Fourth Dimension, is used to determine "degrees" or planes.

This fourth dimension can be called "Vibration". It is a well known fact both in modern science and among hermeticists, who have encapsulated this truth in their third principle: "everything is in motion, everything vibrates, nothing is at rest". From the highest manifestation to the lowest, all things vibrate. And not only do they vibrate with different intensities, but also in different dimensions and in different ways. The degrees of vibrational "intensity" constitute the measurement levels on the scale of vibrations, in other words, the degrees of the Fourth Dimension. All these degrees make up what occultists call "planes".

The higher the degree of vibration, the higher the plane. So, although a plane is not a place or a state or condition, it possesses qualities common to both. We will have more to say about vibrations in the upcoming chapters when we study the hermetic principle of Vibration.

However, it is worth remembering that the three great planes are not real and concrete divisions of the phenomena of the Universe but rather arbitrary means used by the hermetists to aid in the thought and study of the various degrees and forms of universal activity and life. The atom of matter, the unit of force, the human mind, and the being of the archangel are all but degrees on one and the same scale, and all are fundamentally equal, with the difference simply being a matter of degree and vibrational intensity. They are all creations of the ALL and have their existence within its infinite mind.

The hermetists subdivide each of these three great planes into seven lesser planes, and each of these into seven subplanes. These divisions are more or less arbitrary and interconnect with each other, but have been adopted for the convenience of scientific study.

The Grand Physical Plane, along with its seven lesser planes, is the division that encompasses all phenomena of the universe related to things, forces, and physical manifestations. It includes all forms of what we know as matter, as well as all forms of what we call energy or force. However, it should be noted that Hermetic Philosophy does not recognize matter as something in itself, nor as if it had a separate existence from the mind of the ALL. The premise is that matter is nothing more than a form of energy, that is, an energy of a certain kind with a lower vibratory intensity. And according to this, the hermeticists classify matter under the heading of energy and assign it three of the seven lesser planes of the Grand Physical Plane.

These seven lesser divisions are as follows:

I. The plane of matter (A)

II. The plane of matter (B)

III. The plane of matter (C)

IV. The plane of ethereal substance.

V. The plane of energy (A)

VI. The plane of energy (B)

VII. The plane of energy (C)

The Plane of Matter A encompasses solid, liquid, and gaseous material forms, as generally recognized in physical texts. The Plane of Matter B comprises certain higher and subtler forms of existence that science is just beginning to understand: phenomena of radiant matter, such as radium, which belong to the lowest subdivision of this lesser plane. The Plane of Matter C includes forms of even more subtle and tenuous matter, the existence of which is not even suspected by current scientists. The Plane of Ethereal Substance encompasses what science calls "ether", an extremely tenuous and elastic substance that pervades all Universal Space and acts as a medium for the transmission of energy waves such as light, heat, electricity, among others. This ethereal substance serves as the link between what we call matter and energy, sharing the nature of both. According to Hermetic doctrine, this plane has seven subdivisions, like the other lesser planes, and, in reality, there are seven ethers instead of one.

Next is the Plane of Energy A, which encompasses the forms of energy commonly recognized by science, and its seven subdivisions are heat, light, magnetism, electricity, attraction (gravitation, cohesion, chemical affinity, etc.), and other forms of force that scientific experiments reveal but have not yet been named or classified. The Plane of Energy B comprises seven subdivisions of the higher modalities of energy that science has not yet discovered but have been termed "The Subtle Forces of Nature". These forces manifest through certain mental phenomena made possible by them. The Plane of Energy C encompasses seven subdivisions of highly organized energy that possess many life like characteristics but are not recognized by humans in their current state of development, as they are only usable by beings on the Spiritual Plane. This energy is inconceivable and can be considered almost as "divine power". Beings that utilize it are like gods, even when compared to the highest humans we know.

The Great Mental Plane encompasses the forms of living beings we know in our everyday life, as well as other less known forms, except for occultists.

The classification of the seven minor mental planes is not entirely satisfactory; it is rather arbitrary (unless accompanied by complicated explanations that are not relevant to the purpose of this book), but we will briefly mention them.

I. The plane of mineral mind

II. The plane of elemental mind (A)

III. The plane of vegetable mind

IV. The plane of elemental mind (B)

V. The plane of animal mind

VI. The plane of elemental mind (C)

VII. The plane of human mind

The Plane of Mineral Mind encompasses the states or conditions of the units, entities, groups, and combinations that animate the forms known as minerals and chemicals. These entities should not be confused with molecules, atoms, and particles, as the latter are merely the material body of these entities, just as the human body is only its material form and not the being itself. In a sense, these entities can be called "souls", and they are living beings with a very limited degree of development, life, and mentality, barely a little more than the units of "living energy" that make up the higher subdivisions of the higher physical plane. Commonly, people do not attribute mind, soul, or life to the mineral kingdom, but all occultists recognize their existence, and modern science is rapidly approaching this perspective. Molecules, atoms, and particles have their own preferences and aversions, likes and dislikes, attractions and repulsions, affinities and non affinities, etc., and some scientists have expressed the opinion that atoms have desires, will, emotions, and feelings that differ only in degree from those of humans. We do not have space to discuss this matter here, but all occultists know it to be a fact, and others refer to the latest scientific discoveries as corroboration. This plane is divided into seven subdivisions, as is customary.

The Plane of Elemental Mind A encompasses the state, condition, and degree of mental and vital development of a class of entities unknown to the common man but known to occultists. They are invisible to the ordinary senses of human beings but exist and play their part in the Drama of the Universe. Their level of intelligence lies between the entities of the mineral and chemical kingdoms on one hand and the entities of the animal kingdom on the other. There are also seven subdivisions on this plane.

The Plane of Vegetable Mind and its seven subdivisions encompass the states or conditions of the entities that make up the plant kingdom, including the mental and vital phenomena that are commonly known. In recent times, many interesting scientific works have been written about the mind and life in plants. Vegetables possess life, mind, and soul, just like animals, humans, and superhuman beings.

The Plane of Elemental Mind B and its seven subdivisions encompass the states and conditions of a form of elementals or invisible entities that play their role in the Universe. Their mind and vitality are part of the scale between the Plane of Vegetable Mind and the Plane of Animal Mind, and these entities partake in the nature of both.

The Plane of Animal Mind and its seven subdivisions encompass the states and conditions of the entities, beings, or souls that animate the living bodies of animals and are known to all. It is not necessary to go into details about this realm or plane of life, as the animal world is as familiar to us as our own.

The Plane of Elemental Mind C and its seven subdivisions encompass the entities or invisible beings that partake in the nature of animal and human life to some degree and combination. The elements belonging to this plane, found at its highest level, possess a semi human intelligence.

The Plane of the Human Mind and its seven subdivisions encompasses the manifestations of life and mentality that are common to the human being in its various degrees and divisions. At this point, it should be noted that the average person occupies the fourth subdivision of the Plane of the Human Mind, and only the most intelligent have crossed the boundaries of the fifth subdivision. The human race has spent millions of years to reach this level and will take many more years to reach the sixth and seventh subdivisions. However, it should be remembered that there have been races before ours that have gone through these grades and have advanced beyond them. Our own race is the fifth (with some laggards from the fourth) that treads the Path. In it, there have been some advanced souls who have surpassed the majority and have reached the sixth and even the seventh subdivision, and some have gone even further. The human of the sixth subdivision will be the superhuman, and that of the seventh will be the ultra-human.

When considering the seven lesser mental planes, we have made a general reference to the three elemental planes. We do not wish to delve into further details in this work, as the subject does not belong to this plane of philosophy and general teachings. However, we have mentioned this to provide a clearer idea of the relationships between these planes and those with which we are more familiar. The Elemental Planes bear the same relationship in terms of mentality and vitality to the Mineral, Vegetable, Animal, and Human Planes as the black keys on a piano do to the white keys. The white keys are sufficient to produce music, but there are certain scales, melodies, and harmonies in which the black keys play their part, and their presence is necessary. They are also necessary as connecting links between the different states of being on the other planes, thus allowing certain forms of development. This fact will provide readers who can read between the lines with a new understanding of the process of evolution, a new key to the secret door of life hidden between kingdom and kingdom. All occultists have a profound knowledge of these great realms of the Elementals, and esoteric works are full of references to them.

Those who have read "Zanoni" by Bulwer Lytton[12] and other similar legends will recognize these entities belonging to the mentioned planes of life.

---

12 "Zanoni" is a novel written by Edward Bulwer Lytton that combines elements of romance, mysticism, and occultism. Set in 18thcentury Europe, the story follows Zanoni, an immortal who possesses hidden knowledge and powers, and his love for a mortal woman. The work addresses themes such as the pursuit of spiritual knowledge and the struggle between earthly love and transcendence. "Zanoni" has been considered a precursor to esoteric literature and has left a lasting mark on the genre.

As we delve into the Great Spiritual Plane, we face a challenge: how to explain and comprehend those higher states of existence, life, and mentality to minds incapable of conceiving the higher subdivisions of the Human Mental Plane? It is an impossible task. We can only speak in general terms. How to describe light to someone blind from birth? How to explain the taste of sugar to someone who has never tasted sweetness? How to convey harmony to a person who is deaf?

All we can say is that the seven lesser planes of the Great Spiritual Plane (each with their usual seven subdivisions) harbor beings who are as superior to the current human being as the latter is superior to a worm or even lower life forms. The life of these beings transcends ours to such an extent that we can't even imagine the details. Their minds are so elevated that we can barely consider our own thinking, and our mental processes seem to them mere material processes. The matter that makes up their bodies belongs to the highest plane, and some say they are enveloped in pure energy. What can we say about such beings?

In the seven lesser planes of the Great Spiritual Plane, there exist beings we call Angels, Archangels, or demigods. In the lower planes dwell those we call Masters and Adepts. Above them are the great hierarchies of angelic hosts, incomprehensible to humans, and above them are those whom, without disrespect, we could call gods, for their level of elevation on the scale is so high, their power and intelligence so vast, that they surpass all human conceptions of Deity. These beings transcend all that is imaginable, and only the word "Divine" can be applied to them. Many of them, including the angelic hosts, show great interest in the affairs of the Universe and play a fundamental role in the processes of cosmic evolution and progress. Their occasional intervention and direct assistance in human affairs have given rise to numerous legends, beliefs, religions, and traditions of past and present races. They have imprinted their knowledge and power on the world time and time again, always under the law of the ALL.

Nevertheless, these beings of elevated nature exist merely as creations of the mind of the ALL and are subject to cosmic processes and universal laws. While we might call them "gods" if we wish, they are nothing more than our elder brothers: advanced souls who have surpassed their peers and have temporarily foregone the ecstasy of absorption into the ALL to aid the race in its ascent along the Path. However, they belong to the Universe and are subject to its conditions, they are mortal, and their plane is inferior to that of the Absolute Spirit.

Only the most advanced hermetics are capable of comprehending the secret teachings about the states of existence and the powers manifested on the spiritual planes. These phenomena are so superior to what occurs on the Mental Planes that any attempt at description would only cause great confusion. Only those whose minds have been carefully educated in Hermetic Philosophy for years, and those who have brought with them prior knowledge from past incarnations, can fully grasp the meaning of the teachings about the spiritual planes. Many of these teachings are zealously guarded by the hermetics, deeming them too sacred, significant, and even dangerous to be publicly disclosed.

The intelligent student will understand that when the hermetics use the word "Spirit", they refer to "living power", animated force, internal or vital essence, and it should not be confused with the religious or ethereal connotation that is generally attributed to it. The occultist uses the word Spirit in the sense of "animating principle", which implies power, living energy, mystical force, among other aspects. The occultist knows very well that this spiritual power can be used for good or for evil, according to the principle of polarity, a fact recognized by many religions in their concepts of Satan, Beelzebub, the Devil, Lucifer, fallen Angels, etc. For this reason, knowledge about these planes has been kept secret, in the Sanctuary of Sanctuaries of all esoteric fraternities and occult orders. It has been guarded in the innermost chamber of the Temple.

However, we can say this: those who have attained great spiritual powers and used them negatively have created a terrible destiny for themselves. The swing of the pendulum of Rhythm will inevitably take them to the opposite extreme of material existence, from where they will have to traverse the same path again along the multiple spirals of the Path, but always bearing the vibrant memory of the heights from which they fell due to their misdeeds. The legends of the fallen angels have a real basis, as all occultists well know. The selfish struggle for power on the spiritual planes inevitably leads the soul to lose its spiritual balance and fall as far as it had ascended. However, even for these souls, the opportunity to turn back and embark on the journey of return presents itself, paying the tremendous penalty in accordance with the immutable cosmic law.

To conclude, we remind you that, according to the Principle of Correspondence, which embodies the truth that "As above, so below; as below, so above", all seven Hermetic principles are in full operation on the various planes, physical, mental, and spiritual. The Principle of Mentalism applies to all planes since they all exist in the mind of the ALL. The Principle of Correspondence is manifested in all of them, as there is an analogy, agreement, correspondence, and harmony between the different planes. The Principle of Vibration also manifests on all planes, as the differences that separate them result from vibration, as we have explained. The Principle of Polarity is manifested on every plane, with seemingly opposite and contradictory extremes. The Principle of Rhythm is manifested on every plane, with flows and ebbs, ascents and descents, ins and outs. The Principle of Cause and Effect is manifested on every plane, with each effect being the result of a cause, and each cause generating an effect. The Principle of Gender is manifested on every plane, with creative energy expressing and operating through masculine and feminine aspects.

"As above, so below; as below, so above". The age old Hermetic axioms contain the great principles of universal phenomena. As we examine the other principles, we will see more clearly the truth of the universal nature of this great Principle of Correspondence.

CHAPTER IX

VIBRATION

"Nothing rests; everything moves; everything vibrates".
The Kybalion.

The third Great Hermetic Principle, known as the Principle of Vibration, reveals the truth that motion is manifested throughout the Universe. Nothing remains at rest; everything is in constant motion, vibration, and circulation. This principle was recognized by ancient Greek philosophers in their systems but was later forgotten for centuries, except by those who pursued Hermetic teachings. In the 19th century, physical science rediscovered this truth, and the scientific advancements of the 20th century have confirmed and supported this ancient teaching of Hermetic Philosophy.

Hermetic doctrine not only asserts that everything is in constant motion but also that the differences between the various manifestations of universal power are entirely due to different forms and intensities of vibration. Furthermore, the ALL itself manifests a constant vibration of infinite intensity and speed, to the point where it could be considered as if it were at rest. Instructors emphasize to the student the fact that even in the physical plane, an object that rotates rapidly, such as a wheel, appears to be still. Spirit represents one of the poles of vibration, while the other pole is formed by extremely dense forms of matter. Between these two poles, there are countless intensities and modes of vibration.

Modern science has confirmed that everything we call matter and energy is nothing more than different forms of vibratory motion. Even some of the most advanced scientists are rapidly adopting the occultists' viewpoint regarding mental phenomena: that they are simply modes of vibration or motion. Now, let's examine what science has to say about vibrations in matter and energy.

Firstly, science asserts that all manifest matter, to some degree, exhibits vibrations generated by temperature or heat. Whether an object is cold or hot (as both are simply different degrees of the same), it displays certain thermal vibrations and is therefore in a vibratory state. All particles of matter follow a circular motion, whether they be corpuscles or celestial bodies. Planets orbit their suns, and many of them also rotate on their own axis. In turn, suns revolve around larger centers, and it is believed that these, in turn, revolve around even larger ones, and so on, infinitely. The molecules composing any type of matter are in constant vibration, moving around other molecules and colliding with each other. These molecules are made up of atoms, which, like molecules, are also in constant motion and vibration. Atoms are composed of particles, known as "electrons", "ions", among other names, which are also in a state of rapid agitation, revolving around each other with various vibratory modes. In this way, all manifest matter exhibits vibration, in accordance with the corresponding hermetic principle.

And in the same way, it happens with various forms of energy. Science maintains that light, heat, magnetism, and electricity are nothing more than different forms of vibratory motion somehow related to or perhaps emanating from the ether. The nature of the phenomenon known as cohesion, which is the principle of molecular attraction, the chemical affinity, which is the principle of atomic attraction, and gravitation (the greatest enigma of the three), which is the principle of attraction by which every particle or mass of matter is drawn toward any other particle or mass, has not yet been elucidated. These three modalities of energy are still not understood by science, although scholars tend to believe that they are also manifestations of some form of vibratory energy, an idea that the hermetics have taught for long periods in the past.

The universal ether, whose existence science postulates without clearly understanding its nature, had already been explained by the hermetics, who claimed that it was a higher manifestation of what was mistakenly called matter; that is, that ether was matter in a higher degree of vibration. They called it Etheric Substance and argued that this substance was extremely subtle and elastic, filling universal space and acting as a medium for the transmission of vibratory energy waves such as heat, light, electricity, magnetism, among others. Etheric substance is the link that connects the modality of vibratory energy we know as matter on one hand, and the one we know as energy or force on the other, manifesting its own degree of vibration, both in intensity and mode.

Scientists offer an analogy to illustrate the effects of increasing vibration: a wheel spinning at high speed. Suppose the wheel is spinning slowly. In that case, we perceive it as an "object". If the rotation speed is slow, we can easily see it but don't hear any sound. As the speed gradually increases, a low and deep note begins to be heard. As the speed increases, the note rises on the musical scale, and we can distinguish one note after another as the rotation speed increases. Finally, when the motion reaches a certain limit, it reaches the last note perceptible to the human ear. If the speed continues to increase, absolute silence prevails.

Nothing can be heard anymore because the intensity of the movement is so high that the human ear cannot perceive its vibrations.

Then, gradually, different shades of color begin to be perceived. After a while, the eye starts to distinguish a dark red. This red becomes brighter and brighter. If the speed continues to increase, red will transform into orange, orange into yellow. Then come shades of green, blue, and indigo, and finally, the violet hue appears. The speed keeps growing: then all color disappears because the human eye can no longer perceive it. However, certain radiations emanate from the rotating object that the human eye cannot see: the rays used in photography and other subtle radiations of light.

Afterward, Xrays begin to manifest, and later, electricity and magnetism start to generate.

When the object has reached a certain level of vibration, its molecules disintegrate and dissolve into their original elements or atoms. Following the principle of vibration, atoms would separate into countless particles or electrons, of which they are composed. And, finally, even the particles would disappear, and it could be said that the object is composed of ethereal substance. Science does not dare to take the illustration further, but the hermetics assert that if the vibrations continue to increase, the object would successively pass through higher states of manifestation, reaching the mental plane and then the spiritual plane, until it is ultimately absorbed into the ALL, which is the Absolute Spirit. However, long before reaching ethereal substance, the "object" would have ceased to exist as such. Nevertheless, the illustration is correct in demonstrating the effects of the continuous increase in vibrational intensity.

It is important to remember that in the previous illustration, when reaching the states where the object emits color, light, etc., the issue regarding these forms of energy (which are on a much higher level) has not yet been resolved. It simply reaches a level of vibration in which these energies are released to a certain extent from the limitations imposed by molecules, atoms, and particles. These energies, although much higher on the scale compared to matter, are trapped and confined within material combinations due to the forces that manifest through them, using material forms. In this way, they remain confined within their corporeal creations, which is true to some extent for all creation, as the creative force becomes enveloped in its own creation.

However, the Hermetic doctrine goes far beyond modern science and asserts that every manifestation of thought, emotion, reason, will, desire, or any other mental state is accompanied by vibrations, some of which radiate outward and have the power to influence the minds of others through "induction". This is the cause of telepathy, mental influence, and other effects of one mind's power over another, increasingly known thanks to the widespread dissemination of occult works written by disciples and instructors.

Every thought, emotion, or mental state possesses its own intensity and corresponding vibratory mode. These mental states can be reproduced, much like a musical note can be reproduced by vibrating the strings of an instrument at the appropriate speed, or like a particular color can be reproduced. By understanding the Principle of Vibration applied to mental phenomena, one can polarize their mind to the desired degree, thus gaining complete mastery and control over their mental states. Similarly, they can influence the minds of others, inducing in them the desired mental states. In short, they can generate on the Mental Plane what science achieves on the physical plane, that is, vibrations at will. Of course, this power can only be acquired through proper instruction, exercises, and practices, forming part of the science known as "mental transmutation", a branch of Hermetic Philosophy.

A reflection on what has been discussed will reveal that the Principle of Vibration is present in all the marvelous phenomena of the powers manifested by the Masters and Adepts, who seemingly can evade the laws of nature but, in reality, only employ one law against another, one principle against others, achieving their results by modifying the vibrations of material things or energies. This is how they carry out what we commonly call miracles.

As one of the oldest Hermetic authorities said, “One who has understood the Principle of Vibration has attained the scepter of Power”.

CHAPTER X

POLARITY

"Everything in the universe is dual, has opposite poles; there are pairs of opposites. Like and unlike are the same essence; opposites are identical in nature, only differing in degree. Extremes are connected to each other; all truths are partially true, all paradoxes can be reconciled".

The Kybalion.

The Fourth Great Hermetic Principle, the Principle of Polarity, reveals the truth that all manifestations have two faces, two aspects, two poles; a pair of opposites with countless degrees between them. The ancient paradoxes that have confounded the human mind find explanation when understanding this principle. Throughout history, humans have recognized something akin to this principle and have attempted to express it through sayings, maxims, or aphorisms such as the following: "Everything is and is not at the same time"; "all truths are half truths"; "every truth is half false"; "all things have two faces"; "there is always a reverse to every obverse", among others.

The Hermetic teachings maintain that the apparent difference between opposing things is only a matter of degree. They assert that every pair of opposites can be reconciled and that the thesis and antithesis are identical in nature, differing only in degree. The universal reconciliation of opposites is achieved by recognizing this Principle of Polarity. Examples of this principle can be found everywhere once the true nature of things is examined.

Spirit and matter are simply the poles of the same reality, and the intermediate planes are only different vibrational degrees. The ALL and the many are the same; the difference lies solely in the degree of mental manifestation. In this way, the LAW and the laws are the two poles of a single reality. The same applies to the PRINCIPLE and the principles, the infinite MIND and the finite mind.

If we delve into the physical plane, we find that heat and cold are of identical nature, with the difference being merely a matter of degrees. The thermometer indicates different temperature levels, with the lower pole known as "cold" and the upper pole as "heat". Between them, there are multiple degrees of heat and cold, and any name attributed to them is valid. Of two degrees, the upper one is always hotter compared to the lower one, which is colder. There is no specific point on the thermometer where heat ceases and cold begins absolutely. It all comes down to higher or lower vibrations. Even the words "high" and "low" we use are simply poles of the same thing, as the terms are relative. The same goes for "East" and "West". If we travel around the world in an eastward direction, eventually, we will reach a point we call west, considering it from the starting point. If we head far enough north, we will soon be traveling south, and vice versa.

Light and darkness are poles of the same reality, with multiple intermediate degrees. The same occurs in the musical scale. Starting from a C, we progress and find another C, and so on, with the differences between the extremes simply being a matter of degrees. In the color scale, something similar happens, where the only difference between red and violet is the vibrational intensity. Big and small are relative concepts. The same goes for loudness and quietness, hard and soft, sharp and dull. Positive and negative are two poles of the same reality, with countless gradations between them.

The concept of good and bad is not absolute; what we consider good at one end, we call bad at the other, or good in one and bad in the other, depending on the sense we want to attribute to it. One thing is less good than the one that stands above it on the scale, but, in turn, that less good thing can be better in comparison to the one that has a degree more or less depending on its position on the scale.

The same occurs on the mental plane. Love and hate are considered as diametrical opposites, completely different and irreconcilable. However, if we apply the Principle of Polarity, we discover that there is no absolute love or absolute hate, distinct and separate from each other. Both terms are simply applied to the two poles of the same reality. If we start at any point on the scale, we will find "more love" or "less hate" as we move upwards, or "less love" as we move downwards, and this holds true regardless of the starting point we choose, whether it is high or low.

There are numerous degrees of love and hate, and there even exists an intermediate point where liking and disliking blend in such a way that it becomes impossible to distinguish them. Courage and fear also follow the same rule. Pairs of opposites are present everywhere. Wherever we find one thing, we will also find its opposite: the two poles.

This fact is what allows the hermeticist to transform one mental state into another, transmuting along the lines of polarization. Things of different natures cannot transmute into each other, but those of the same nature can. Thus, love cannot become east or west, nor red or violet, but it can transform into hate, and likewise, hate can become love by changing its polarity. Courage can transmute into fear, and vice versa. Hard things can become soft, hot things can become cold, and so on. Transmutation always occurs between things of the same nature but different degree.

In the case of a cowardly man, if he raises his mental vibrations along the line of fear courage, he will fill himself with bravery and contempt for danger. Similarly, a lazy person can become active and energetic simply by polarizing along the lines of the desired quality.

Disciples familiar with the methods used by various schools of mental science to induce changes in the mental states of their followers may not easily grasp the underlying principle behind these changes. However, once the Principle of Polarity is understood, it is immediately clear that these mental changes are caused by a change in polarity, a sliding along the same scale. This change does not involve transforming one thing into something entirely different but rather amounts to a simple shift in the degree of the same thing, which is a significant difference. For example, taking an example from the physical world, it is impossible to turn heat into sharpness, heaviness, elevation, etc., but it can be easily transmuted into cold by dampening the vibration. Similarly, hatred and love are mutually transmutable, as are fear and courage. However, fear cannot be transformed into love, nor courage into hatred. Mental states belong to countless categories, each of which has its opposite poles along which transmutation is possible.

It will be easily understood that in both mental states and phenomena of the physical plane, the two poles can be classified as positive and negative, respectively. Thus, love is positive compared to hatred; courage compared to fear; activity compared to inertia, and so on. Even without knowing the principle of vibration, it is noticeable that the positive pole appears to be of a higher degree than the negative and has the ability to easily dominate it. The tendency of nature is toward the dominant activity of the positive pole.

In addition to changing the poles of one's own mental states through the application of the art of polarization, the phenomenon of mental influence, in its various forms, demonstrates that the principle can be extended to the phenomena of one mind influencing another, a topic that has been extensively studied in recent years. When it is understood that mental induction is possible, meaning that mental states can be induced by others, one can see how a certain kind of vibration or polarity can be communicated to another mind, thus changing the polarization of the mind as a whole. Most of the results obtained through "mental treatments" are achieved through this principle. For example, let's assume that a person is sad, melancholic, and full of fears. A scientist of the mind elevates their own mentality to the desired degree of vibration through their previously trained willpower and, in this way, achieves the required polarization in their own mentality. Then, through induction, they produce a similar mental state in the other individual, resulting in an increase in the vibrations of the latter and a polarization toward the positive pole of the scale instead of the negative pole. Their fears, melancholy, etc., are transformed into courage, joy, and similar internal states. A little reflection on this subject will demonstrate that these mental changes primarily occur along the lines of polarization, being more a matter of change than of class.

The knowledge of this great Hermetic principle provides us with a better understanding of our own mental states and those of others. We will realize that these states are simply matters of degree, and by recognizing this fact, we can raise our internal vibrations at will, changing our polarity and becoming masters of our thoughts rather than being slaves and servants to them. This knowledge will also enable us to intelligently assist others by changing their polarity through proper methods. It is highly beneficial to become familiar with this principle, as a precise understanding will shed a great deal of light on difficult and obscure problems.

CHAPTER XI

RHYTHM

"Everything flows and ebbs, everything moves and fluctuates, everything rises and falls; the pendulum swing is evident in all manifestations; the movement to the right is equal to the movement to the left; Rhythm is the perfect compensation".

The Kybalion.

The Fifth Great Hermetic Principle, the Principle of Rhythm, reveals the truth that in everything that exists, there is a measured oscillation, a back and forth movement, a ebb and flow like a pendulum, a tide with its rises and falls, always present in the physical, mental, and spiritual planes. The Principle of Rhythm is closely connected to the Principle of Polarity mentioned earlier. Rhythm manifests itself between the two poles established by the principle of polarity. However, this does not imply that rhythmic oscillation reaches the extremes of each pole, as this rarely happens. In fact, it is difficult to establish the opposite poles in their fullest expression in most cases.

Nevertheless, the oscillation always moves first towards one pole and then towards the other. There is always an action and a reaction, a forward and a backward movement, an ascent and a descent, present in all things and phenomena in the universe. From masses and worlds to human beings, animals, plants, minerals, energies, forces, mind and matter, and even spirit, all manifest this principle. It becomes evident in the creation and destruction of worlds, in the rise and fall of nations, in the history of the life of all things, and ultimately in the mental states of human beings.

From the manifestations of the Spirit, the All, it can be observed that there is always an emission followed by absorption, a breath and an aspiration of Brahma, as the Brahmins say. Universes are created, reach their lowest point of materiality, and then the oscillation of return begins. Suns are born, reach their maximum power, start their backward progression, and, after countless eons, become inert masses of matter, waiting for a new impulse to infuse them with new internal energies to start a new cycle of solar life. And this happens with all worlds: they are born, grow, and die, only to be reborn once again. The same occurs with all things with form or body: they oscillate from action to reaction, from birth to death, from activity to inactivity, and the cycle begins anew. The same is true for great philosophical movements, beliefs of all kinds, governments, nations, etc.: they are born, grow, reach maturity, decline, die, only to be reborn again.

The pendulum oscillation is evident everywhere.

Night follows day, and day follows night. The pendulum swings from summer to winter and vice versa. Corpuscles, atoms, and molecules, like all masses of matter, oscillate in the circle corresponding to their nature. There is no absolute rest or complete cessation of movement. Every motion participates in rhythm. This principle has universal application. It can be applied to any question or phenomenon in the multifaceted aspects of life. It can be applied to all manifestations of human activity. There is always a rhythmic oscillation from one pole to another. The universal pendulum is always in motion. The tides of life ebb and flow according to the law.

Modern science acknowledges the principle of rhythm and considers it universally applicable to material things. However, the hermeticists go much further and understand that its manifestations also extend to the mental activities of human beings, thus explaining the succession of moods, emotions, and other impactful changes that we experience within ourselves. By studying the operation of this principle, the hermeticists have discovered how to free themselves from these activities through transmutation.

The Hermetic Masters discovered that, although the principle of rhythm was constant and evident in all mental phenomena, there were two planes of manifestation when it came to these phenomena. They found that there were two general planes of consciousness: the Lower and the Higher. This discovery allowed them to ascend to the higher plane and thus escape the oscillation of the rhythmic pendulum that manifested on the lower plane. In other words, the pendulum's oscillation occurs in the unconscious plane, and consciousness is not affected by it. They called this law the Law of Neutralization. Its operation involves elevating the Self above the vibrations of the unconscious plane of mental activity, so that the negative swing of the pendulum does not manifest in consciousness and does not affect us. It's like rising above something and letting it pass beneath you. The Hermetic instructor or disciple polarizes themselves at the required pole and, through a similar process of "denying" participation in the backward swing or, if you prefer, "denying" its influence on them, they firmly hold their polarized position, allowing the mental pendulum to swing back in the unconscious plane. Every human being who has gained some self-mastery does this to a greater or lesser extent, preventing negative mental states from affecting them, applying the law of neutralization. However, the master takes this to a much higher level of effectiveness and mastery, achieving a level of mental equilibrium and inflexibility that is almost unimaginable to those who are carried away by the mental pendulum of their emotions and moods.

Any thoughtful person will rightly appreciate the great importance of this subject when considering how most individuals are slaves to their own moods, feelings, and emotions, and how little self-mastery they have. Just a bit of reflection is enough to understand how much those rhythmical oscillations have affected our lives, how a period of enthusiasm is followed by one of depression. Similarly, we experience periods of courage followed by periods of discouragement and fear. This happens to everyone, or at least to the majority: our emotions and feelings rise and fall, but we never suspect the cause of this phenomenon. If we understand how this principle operates, we will gain the key to mastering these fluctuations and will come to know our own nature much better, avoiding being carried away by these fluctuations. Willpower is much more powerful than the conscious manifestation of this principle, although the principle itself can never be destroyed. We can free ourselves from its effects, but the principle will continue to operate. The pendulum always swings, but we can avoid being swept away by its motion.

Furthermore, there are other peculiarities in the operation of this Principle of Rhythm that we will now discuss. Within its functioning is what is known as the law of compensation. One of the definitions or meanings of the word "compensation" is "to balance" or "counteract", and in this sense, the term is used in Hermetic Philosophy. The Kybalion refers to this law of compensation when it says: "The measure of the swing to the right is the same as the swing to the left; rhythm is compensation".

The law of compensation is the one that causes oscillation in one direction to generate oscillation in the opposite direction, thereby achieving a mutual balance. In the physical plane, we can observe numerous examples of this law. A clock pendulum swings to the right to a certain point and then swings back to the left to the same extent. The seasons balance in the same way. Tides obey this same law. And this law is manifested in all rhythmical phenomena. If the pendulum only makes a short swing to the right, it will also make a short swing to the left. If the swing to the right is wide, the swing to the left will be equally wide. An object thrown upwards must follow exactly the same path back. The force with which a projectile is launched upwards is reproduced when the projectile returns to Earth. This law is constant in the physical plane, as any reference to the highest scientific authority will confirm.

But the hermetic goes further and asserts that mental states are subject to the same law. The individual capable of experiencing great pleasure will also be capable of suffering to an equal extent. Those who can only experience mild pain will also not be able to enjoy great pleasure. The pig suffers very little on a mental level, but at the same time, it cannot experience great enjoyment: there is a balance. On the other hand, there are animals that experience extraordinary joy, but their nervous system and temperament also subject them to extreme degrees of pain. The same applies to the human being. There are temperaments that can only experience limited joy, but then they only have the capacity to endure minimal pain, while others can enjoy intensely but also suffer to the same extent. The rule is that the capacity to experience pleasure and pain in each individual is balanced. The law of compensation operates widely in this aspect as well.

But the hermetic goes further in this matter and asserts that before we can experience a degree of pleasure, it is necessary to have oscillated proportionally towards the other pole of feeling or sensation. The negative in this realm precedes the positive. This means that experiencing a certain degree of pleasure does not necessarily imply that we "have to pay for it" with a corresponding degree of pain. On the contrary, pleasure is the rhythmic oscillation, in accordance with the law of compensation, that arises from a degree of pain experienced previously, whether in the current life or in past incarnations. This sheds a new perspective on the problem of pain.

The Hermetics view the chain of lives as continuous, as simple stages of an individual's one life. In this way, rhythmic oscillation is interpreted as such and would make no sense if the doctrine of reincarnation were not accepted.

Furthermore, the Hermetic maintains that the master or advanced disciple is capable, to a supreme degree, of avoiding oscillation toward pain by carrying out the process of neutralization mentioned earlier. By ascending to the higher plane of the Self, many of the experiences that affect those who dwell on lower planes are avoided.

The law of compensation plays a significant role in the lives of human beings, as it is evident that one generally pays the price for what one has or lacks. If you possess something, you lack something else, and thus the balance is maintained. No one can keep their penny and have the cake at the same time; everything has its pleasant and unpleasant aspect. What one gains is always paid for by what one loses. The wealthy possess many things that the poor lack, while the poor have things that are often beyond the reach of the wealthy. The millionaire who enjoys feasts and has the fortune to satisfy their desires and gluttony lacks the appetite necessary to enjoy them, and envies the appetite and digestion of the laborer who lacks the fortune and inclination of the millionaire, finding more pleasure in their simple meal than the millionaire with no appetite and a ruined stomach. And so it goes with everything in life. The law of compensation is always in action, constantly balancing and counteracting things in the succession of time, although the oscillation of rhythm may span entire lifetimes.

CHAPTER XII

CAUSALITY

"Every cause has its effect, and every effect has its cause; everything happens according to law. Chance is but a name for law unrecognized; there are many planes of causation, but none escapes the law".

The Kybalion.

The Sixth Great Hermetic Principle, known as the Principle of Cause and Effect, holds the truth that nothing happens by chance. Chance is merely a term denoting the existence of an unrecognized or unperceived cause. This principle manifests continuously, without interruptions.

The Principle of Cause and Effect has been fundamental in all scientific thought, whether ancient or modern, and was elucidated by the Hermetic Instructors in ancient times.

While there have been numerous discussions and debates among different schools of thought, these disputes have mainly focused on the details of how this principle operates and the meaning of certain words. However, the inherent principle of Cause and Effect has been accepted as valid by all true thinkers of the world. To consider otherwise would be to remove the phenomenon from the domain of law and order in the universe, relegating it to something imaginary that humanity has named chance.

A brief reflection would reveal that there is actually no such thing as chance. Webster defines chance as "a supposed agent or mode of activity other than a force, law, or purpose; the operation or activity of such an agent; the supposed effect of such an agent; an event, a fortuitous thing, a contingency, etc". However, a deeper reflection will show that there cannot be a casual agent in the sense of something external and outside the law, something separate from cause and effect.

How could there exist something in the phenomenal universe that acts independently of its laws, its order, and its continuity? Such an agent would be completely alien to the harmonious flow of the universe and, therefore, superior to it. We cannot conceive of something outside of the ALL, beyond the law, and this is because the ALL is precisely the law itself. There is no place in the universe for anything external or independent of the law. The existence of something like that would disrupt all natural laws and plunge the universe into utter chaos.

A careful analysis will demonstrate that what we call chance is simply an expression referring to hidden causes, causes that we cannot perceive, causes that we cannot comprehend. The term "chance" comes from the phrase "rolling the dice", implying the idea that the outcome is merely an event without any relation to a specific cause. And it is in this sense that the word is often used. However, when examined closely, it becomes evident that there is no such chance at all in the rolling of a die. Every time the die falls, showing a specific number, it obeys a law as infallible as the one governing the revolution of planets around the Sun. After the die has fallen, there are causes, or chains of causes, links in an unbroken succession that escapes the comprehension of the mind. The position of the die in the hand, the amount of muscular energy used to throw it, the state of the table's surface, all are causes that have their observable effect. But beyond them, there is a concatenation of invisible preceding causes, all of which act on the number that the die will display on its upper face.

If dice are rolled a large number of times, it can be observed that the number of points marked is practically equal, meaning there will be approximately the same number of ones, twos, etc. When tossing a coin into the air, upon landing, it can show heads or tails. However, if tossed a sufficient number of times, the outcome will balance out between heads and tails. All of this is governed by the Law of Cause and Effect, and if we could examine the chain of causes in detail, we would clearly see that it was simply impossible for the die to fall any other way under the same circumstances and at the same moment. If the causes are the same, the result will always be the same. Every event has its cause and its reason. Nothing happens without a cause, or rather, without a chain of causes.

When considering this principle, many become confused because they cannot explain how one thing can be the cause of another, that is, be the creator of the second. In reality, nothing can produce or create another. Cause and effect reside solely in events. An event is what happens, arrives, or occurs as a consequence or result of a previous event. No event creates another; it is simply the preceding link in the vast, coordinated chain of events that flow from the creative energy of the ALL. There is a continuity of links between all preceding, subsequent, and subsequent events. If a stone dislodges from the mountain and falls onto the roof of a farmhouse in the neighboring valley, it may appear to be a random occurrence at first glance, but upon closer examination, an extensive chain of causes will be found behind that event. First, there is the rain that softened the earth holding the stone, allowing it to fall; before that cause, there is the prior influence of the sun and other rains that gradually disintegrated the stone from the rock; even before that, there are the causes that contributed to or originated the formation of the mountain and its successive elevation due to the convulsions of nature, and so on, *ad infinitum*.

If we pause to consider the causes of rain, we can delve into the complexity of the existence of a roof. In short, we would find ourselves immersed in a labyrinth of causes and effects from which it would be difficult to escape.

Just as a man has two parents, four grandparents, eight great grandparents, and so on, reaching millions of ancestors after forty generations, the same happens with the number of causes behind an apparently insignificant event or phenomenon, like the displacement of a light piece of coal carried by the wind. It is not an easy task to trace the path of that speck of soot back to the remote periods in the history of the world when it was part of a sturdy trunk that later turned into coal, and so on, until the moment it flies past us in search of new adventures. A powerful chain of events, of causes and effects, has brought it to its current state, and this is just one of the many events in the chain that will continue generating more events over hundreds and hundreds of years from now. One of the series of events originated by that tiny floating speck of soot has been the writing of these lines, which has required the work of a typographer; this will arouse certain thoughts in your minds, as well as in the minds of others, which in turn will affect others, and so on, to where the mind cannot reach, all because of the simplicity of a speck of soot, demonstrating the relativity and interconnectedness of things and the conclusion that nothing is large or small in the mind that created it.

Let's take a moment to reflect. If, in the dark Stone Age, a particular man hadn't encountered a particular woman, you, who are now reading these lines, wouldn't be here at this moment. And if, perhaps, that same couple hadn't met, we, who write these words, wouldn't be here either. And the simple fact that we, on our part, write and that you read, will not only affect our own lives but will also have a direct or indirect effect on many other people who are alive today or will live in the ages to come. Every thought that arises in our minds, every action we take, has its direct and indirect results, intricately woven together in the grand chain of Cause and Effect.

We do not wish to delve into the discussion of free will and determinism in this work, for multiple reasons. Among them, the main one is that neither of the two aspects is entirely accurate, as both are partially true according to Hermetic teachings. The Principle of Polarity demonstrates that both aspects are half truths, opposite poles of the truth. The truth is that a human being can be simultaneously free and constrained by necessity, depending on the meaning of the terms and the level of truth from which the matter is examined. Ancient writers expressed this point by saying that "the further creation is from the Center, the more limited it is; the closer it is to the Center, the freer it is".

The majority of men are, to a large extent, slaves to inheritance, environment, and other circumstances, and they show very little free will. They are carried away by the opinions, customs, and thoughts of the external world, as well as by their own emotions, feelings, and moods. They do not demonstrate true self-mastery worthy of the name. And, with indignation, they reject this assertion, saying, "I can act with full freedom and do as I please; I do exactly what I want to do". But they cannot explain why or where that sense of "necessity" and "liking" comes from. What makes them prefer one thing over another? What drives them to "like" something and not another? Is there no "reason" behind their "likes" and "needs"? The master can transform "likes" and "needs" into their mental opposite pole. They can and have the ability to "will to will" instead of merely desiring something because some feeling, mood, emotion, or environmental influence arouses in them an inclination or desire to do something specific.

The majority of men are dragged as if they were stones, obeying their environment, external influences, and their own desires, emotions, and internal states, not to mention the desires and wills of others who are stronger. Inheritance, environment, and suggestions carry them along without offering the slightest resistance on their part, without exercising their will in any way. They move like pieces on the chessboard of life, playing their part and remaining on the sidelines after the game. But the Masters, who know the rules of the game, rise above the plane of material life and, by connecting with the higher powers of their own natures, master their own moods, characters, qualities, and polarities, as well as the environment around them. They thus become directors of the game instead of mere pieces: Causes instead of Effects. The Masters do not escape causality on the higher planes but are under the control of these higher laws, and by using these laws; they become owners of circumstances on the lower planes. In this way, they become a conscious part of the Law instead of being its blind instruments. While they obey and serve on the Higher Planes, they dominate and own the material plane.

But both above and below, the Law is always in action. There is no such thing as chance or randomness. The blind goddess has been banished by reason. Now we can see, with eyes illuminated by knowledge, that everything is governed by universal law, and the countless number of laws are nothing more than manifestations of the Great One Law: the Law that encompasses all. It is true that not even a sparrow escapes the Mind of the All, and even the hairs of our head are numbered, as the scriptures say. Nothing exists outside of the law; nothing happens against it. However, let us not fall into the error of considering man as a blind automaton, quite the contrary. The Hermetic doctrine affirms that man can use the

Law against the laws, that the higher will always prevail over the lower, until man reaches a state in which he will seek refuge in his OWN LAW and can escape from all phenomenal laws. Can we comprehend the deep and inner meaning of this?

CHAPTER XIII

GENDER

"Gender is in everything; everything has its masculine and feminine principle; gender manifests on all planes".

The Kybalion.

The Seventh Great Hermetic Principle, the Principle of Gender, reveals the truth that gender is manifested in all things. The masculine and feminine principles are always active in every phenomenon and on all planes of life. It is important to note that the term "gender" in the hermetic sense is not the same as sex in its ordinary meaning.

The word "gender" derives from a Latin root that means to conceive, procreate, generate, create, produce. Upon reflecting on this subject, one understands that this word has a much broader and general meaning than the term "sex", which refers to the physical differences between males and females. Sex is simply a manifestation of Gender on a specific plane of the Great Physical Plane: that of organic life. It is important to note this distinction, as some writers with knowledge of Hermetic principles have attempted to associate this seventh principle with ridiculous and sometimes objectionable theories and teachings related to sex.

The function of Gender is simply to create, produce, generate, etc., and its manifestations are visible on all phenomenal planes. It is somewhat challenging to provide scientific evidence along these lines since science has not yet recognized this principle as universally applicable. However, some evidence is emerging from scientific sources. Firstly, we find a distinct manifestation of the Principle of Gender among the particles, ions, or electrons, which are the building blocks of matter according to current scientific recognition, and when they combine, they form the atom, which was previously considered as the ultimate and indivisible point.

Current science maintains that the atom is composed of a multitude of particles, electrons, or ions (various names for the same entity), which spin and vibrate intensely. Furthermore, it is postulated that the formation of the atom is due to the fact that the negative particles revolve around a positive one. The positive particles seem to exert a certain influence over the negative ones, propelling them to form certain combinations that result in the "creation" or "generation" of an atom. This idea aligns perfectly with the ancient Hermetic teachings, which have always identified the masculine principle of gender with the "positive" and the feminine with the "negative", as in the case of electricity, for example.

It is important to note that the general public has developed a completely erroneous impression of the qualities of the so called "negative pole" of electrified or magnetized matter. The terms positive and negative have been inadequately applied to this phenomenon. The word "positive" implies something real and strong in contrast to the unreality or weakness of the negative. But nothing could be further from the actual facts of electrical phenomena. The negative pole of a battery is, in reality, the pole through which the generation or production of new forms and energies manifests itself. There is nothing "negative" about it. The most respected scientists today use the word "cathode" instead of "negative", derived from a Greek root meaning "to descend, path or way of generation", etc. From the cathode emerge whirlwinds of electrons or particles; from this very pole arise the marvelous "rays" that have revolutionized scientific conceptions in the last decade. The cathode pole is the source of all the strange phenomena that have rendered obsolete the old textbooks and relegated long accepted theories to the heap of discarded scientific speculations. The cathode, or negative pole, is the mother principle of electrical phenomena and the subtlest forms of matter known to science today. Therefore, there are solid reasons to reject the term "negative" and instead propose the word "feminine" as a replacement. These facts lead us to this conclusion, without considering the Hermetic doctrine at all; therefore, we will use the word "feminine" instead of "negative" when referring to this pole of activity.

The latest scientific teachings affirm that the creative corpuscles or electrons are Feminine (science says "composed of negative electricity", we say composed of Feminine energy). A Feminine corpuscle detaches, or rather, separates from a Masculine corpuscle and begins a new career. It actively seeks to unite with a Masculine corpuscle, driven by the natural impulse to create new forms of matter or energy. One writer even goes so far as to use the term "seeks immediately, by its own will, a union", etc. This separation and union form the basis of most chemical activities in the world. When the Feminine corpuscle unites with a Masculine corpuscle, a certain process is initiated. The Feminine particles vibrate rapidly under the influence of Masculine energy and spin rapidly around the latter. The result is the birth of a new atom. This new atom is actually composed of the union of Masculine and Feminine electrons or corpuscles, but when the union is formed, the atom is a separate entity with certain properties, but it no longer exhibits the property of free electricity. The process of separating or detaching Feminine electrons is called "ionization".

These electrons, or corpuscles, are the most active workers in the field of Nature. Various phenomena such as light, heat, electricity, magnetism, attraction, repulsion, chemical affinity, and its opposite, and similar phenomena all arise from the combinations and unions of these corpuscles. And all of this emerges from the operation of the Principle of Gender on the plane of Energy.

The role of the masculine principle seems to be to direct an inherent energy toward the feminine principle, thus activating the creative process. However, it is the feminine principle that always carries out the active work of creation on all planes without exception. Nevertheless, each principle lacks operative energy without the assistance of the other. In some forms of life, both principles combine within a single organism. For this reason, everything in the organic world manifests both genders: the masculine principle is always present in the feminine form. The Hermetic teachings extensively encompass the operation of the two gender principles in the production and manifestation of various forms of energy, etc. It is not necessary to go into detail on this at this time since there is still not enough scientific evidence to support them, as science has not progressed sufficiently. However, the example of electron or corpuscle phenomena demonstrates that science is on the right track and also provides a general idea about the underlying principles.

Some scientific researchers have expressed their belief that in the formation of crystals, there is something resembling a kind of sexual activity, which is another indication of the direction in which the current flows in the field of science.

Each passing year will bring new facts that will corroborate the truth of the Hermetic Principle of Gender. It will be discovered that gender is constantly in action, manifesting in the entire field of inorganic matter as well as in the realm of energy and force. Currently, electricity is regarded as something into which all other forms of energy blend or dissolve. The Electric Theory of the Universe is the latest scientific doctrine put forth and is rapidly gaining popularity and acceptance. From this, it can be stated without fear that if we have been able to find in the phenomenon of electricity, in the very root or source of its manifestations, a clear and evident proof of the presence of gender and its activities, science will ultimately provide evidence of the existence of this great Hermetic principle, the Principle of Gender, in all phenomena of the universe.

There's no need to waste time discussing the well known phenomenon of the "attraction and repulsion" of atoms, chemical affinity, the loves and hatreds of molecules, or the attraction or cohesion between particles of matter. These facts are widely known and require no further commentary. But, has it ever been considered that all these things are simply manifestations of the principle of Gender? Isn't it clear that the phenomenon is universal, whether in corpuscles, molecules, or electrons? Furthermore, isn't it entirely reasonable and logical, as taught in Hermeticism, that the same law of gravitation, that strange attraction by which all particles and bodies in the universe are drawn toward each other, is nothing more than another manifestation of the principle of Gender, operating in the direction of attracting masculine energies to feminine ones and vice versa? Although scientific proof may not be available at present, if we examine the phenomena in the light of Hermetic doctrines on the subject, we will see that there is no better hypothesis than the current one to explain these problems. Let's subject all physical phenomena to scrutiny, and we will see how the principle of Gender becomes evident.

Now let's turn to consider the operation of the Principle on the Mental Plane. There are many interesting characteristics waiting to be examined.

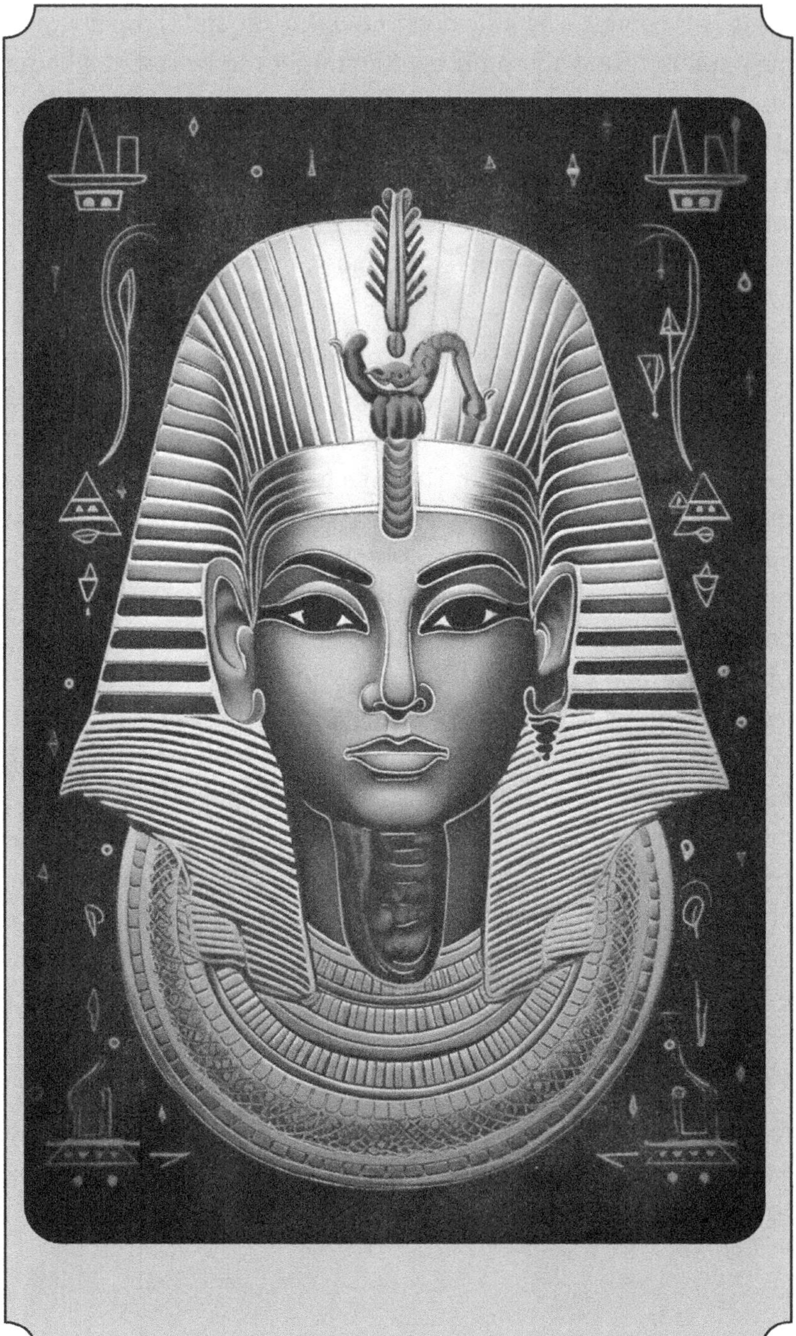

CHAPTER XIV

MENTAL GENDER

Psychology students who have followed the modern trend of thought regarding mental phenomena are impressed by the persistence of the idea of the dual mind, which has manifested so strongly in the last ten or fifteen years and has given rise to a series of plausible theories about the nature and constitution of these "two minds". The late Thomson J. Hudson gained great popularity in 1893 by proposing his well known theory of the "objective and subjective minds", which he claimed existed in each individual. Other writers have attracted almost equal attention with theories about the "conscious and unconscious minds", the "voluntary and involuntary minds", "the active and passive minds", and so on. The theories of various writers may differ from each other, but the underlying principle of "the duality of the mind" persists.

The student of Hermetic philosophy is tempted to smile when reading or hearing about these numerous new theories regarding the duality of the mind, with each school tenaciously clinging to its own doctrine, proclaiming with fervor that it has discovered the truth. If the student peruses the book of hidden history, they will find references from the very beginning to the ancient Hermetic teachings on the principle of gender. And if they continue their examination, they will discover that this ancient philosophy understood the phenomenon of mental duality and explained it through the theory of gender in the mind. This concept of mental gender can be succinctly explained to students who are already familiar with modern theories referring to the same. The masculine principle of the mind corresponds to the so called objective mind, conscious mind, voluntary or active mind, etc., while the feminine principle corresponds to the so called subjective mind, subconscious mind, involuntary, passive mind, etc.

Of course, Hermetic teaching does not align with the many modern theories about the two facets of the mind, nor does it accept many of the facts proclaimed by those schools in support of this dual aspect. We mention this concurrence only to aid the student in assimilating the knowledge previously acquired concerning Hermetic philosophy. Students of Hudson will be familiar with the proposition raised in the second chapter of his work The Law of Psychic Phenomena, which states: "the mystical jargon of the Hermetic philosophers expresses the same general idea"... that is, the duality of the mind. If Dr. Hudson had dedicated more time to deciphering a bit further "the mystical jargon of Hermetic Philosophy", he would have gained much insight into the point of the duality of the mind, but perhaps his most interesting work would not have been written. Now let us consider the Hermetic teachings on mental gender.

The Hermetic Masters impart their teachings on this subject by instructing their students to examine the report of their consciousness about their Being. Students are asked to direct their attention inward, toward the Self that dwells within each of them. They are guided to see that their consciousness first offers them a report of the existence of their Self, and the report is "I Am". This at first appears to be the final word of consciousness, but a closer examination reveals the fact that this "I Am" can be separated or divided into two distinct parts or aspects, which, although they work in unity and together, can still separate in consciousness.

While at first it seems that there is only one "I", a more careful and deeper examination reveals that there is an "I" and a "Me". These mental twins differ in their characteristics and nature, and an examination of their nature and the phenomena that arise from them will shed much light on many of the problems of mental influence.

Let's start with a consideration of the "Me", which is often confused with the "I" by the student, until he delves a bit deeper into the recesses of consciousness. A man thinks of his Self (in its aspect of "Me") as composed of certain feelings, tastes, preferences, dislikes, habits, peculiar bonds, characteristics, etc., which make up his personality, or the "Self" known by himself and by others. He knows that these emotions and feelings change, are born and disappear, are subject to the Principle of Rhythm and the Principle of Polarity, which take him from one extreme of feeling to another. He also considers the "Me" as certain knowledge gathered in his mind, and thus part of himself. This is the "Me" of a human being.

Perhaps we have moved too fast. The "me" of many people is largely made up of their awareness of their own body and physical appetites, etc. And being their consciousness strongly limited to their bodily nature, they practically "live there". Some people go so far in this that they consider their personal appearance as part of their "me" and really see it as a part of themselves. A writer humorously said once that a man is composed of three parts: "Soul, body, and clothes". And this would make many lose their personality if stripped of their clothes. But even those who are not so closely enslaved by the idea of their personal appearance are so by the consciousness of their bodies. They cannot conceive themselves without it. Their mind seems to them "something that belongs" to their body, which, in many cases, is true.

However, as man advances on the scale of consciousness, he acquires the power to separate his "me" from this bodily idea, and can think of his body as something "that belongs" to his mental part. But even then, he is capable of completely identifying the "me" with his mental states, sensations, etc., which he feels exist within him. He will identify these states with himself, rather than considering them just "things" produced by his mentality, that exist in him, come from him, but are not him. He can also find that these states change through volitional effort, and that he is capable of producing a sensation or state of completely opposite nature in the same way, and yet, the same "me" always continues to exist. Over time, he may set aside these various mental states, emotions, feelings, habits, qualities, characteristics, and other personal possessions, considering them as a collection of qualities, curiosities, or valuable possessions of the "not me". This requires great mental concentration and analytical power on the part of the student. But this work is possible, and even those who are not very advanced can see, in their imagination, how the described process is carried out.

After performing that exercise, the disciple will find themselves consciously in possession of a "Being" that can be considered from its dual aspect: the "I" and the "me". The "me" is experienced as something mental where thoughts, ideas, emotions, feelings, and other mental states can arise. It can be seen as the "mental matrix", as the ancients used to say, capable of mental generation. This "me" reveals itself in consciousness as the possessor of latent powers of creation and generation of all kinds. Its capacity for creative energy is immense, as one can feel for themselves. However, it is aware that it must receive some form of energy, either from the same "I", its inseparable companion, or from another "I", in order to carry out its mental creations. This awareness brings with it an understanding of the enormous capacity for mental work and creative power it holds.

The student soon discovers that they are not all there is in their inner consciousness, as they perceive that there exists something mental that can "will" the "me" to act according to a certain creative line, and yet remains apart, as a witness to that mental creation. This part of themselves is given the name "I". And it can rest in consciousness at will. There it is found, not a consciousness of a capacity to generate and create actively in the sense of the gradual process common in mental operations, but rather a consciousness of the capacity to project energy from the "I" to the "me": the "will" that the mental creation begins and progresses.

It is also experienced that the "I" can remain apart, witnessing the mental operations or creations of the "me". This dual aspect exists in the mind of every person: the "I" represents the Masculine Principle of the mental gender, and the "me" represents the Feminine Principle. The "I" embodies the aspect of Being, while the "me" represents the aspect of "becoming". It is observed that the principle of correspondence operates on this plane in the same way as in the creation of the Universe. Both are similar, although they differ enormously in degree. "As above, so below; as below, so above".

These aspects of the mind, the masculine and feminine principles, the "I" and the "me", considered in relation to known psychic and mental phenomena, provide the master key to understanding the operation and manifestation of those nebulous regions of the mind. The principle of mental gender reveals the truth that encompasses the entire field of mental influence phenomena.

The tendency of the feminine principle is always to receive impressions, while the tendency of the masculine principle is to give or express them. The feminine principle has a much wider field of action than the masculine. The feminine principle carries out the work of generating new thoughts, concepts, ideas, and even the work of the imagination. The masculine is content with the act of "willing" in its various phases. However, without the active assistance of the will of the masculine principle, the feminine might content itself with generating mental images that are the result of impressions received from the outside, rather than producing original mental creations.

People who can maintain constant attention on a subject actively use both mental principles: the feminine in the active work of mental generation, and the masculine to stimulate and provide energy to the creative part of the mind. Most barely use the masculine principle and are content to live according to the thoughts and ideas that filter into their "me" and come from the "I" of other minds. However, it is not our purpose to dwell on this aspect of the matter, which can be studied in any good treatise on psychology, keeping in mind the aforementioned key to mental gender.

The student of psychic phenomena is familiar with the reality of the astounding events classified as telepathy, mental influence, suggestion, hypnotism, among others. Many have sought explanations for these various facets of phenomena, following the theories of mental duality promulgated by different instructors. And to a certain extent, they are correct, as there really is a clear and defined manifestation of two distinct phases of mental activity. However, if these students considered that duality in light of the Hermetic teachings on vibration and mental gender, they would discover that the long sought key is within their grasp.

In telepathic phenomena, one can observe how the vibratory energy of the masculine principle is projected towards the feminine principle of another person, who then absorbs this thought and develops and matures it. The same is true for suggestion and hypnotism. The masculine principle of one person emits a suggestion by directing a stream of vibratory energy or power towards the feminine principle of another person. Upon accepting it, the latter assimilates it as their own and thinks accordingly. An idea implanted in another person's mind grows and develops, and over time it is considered as an authentic mental creation of the individual, though in reality, it is but a cuckoo's egg laid in a sparrow's nest, as cuckoos lay their eggs in the nests of others. The normal process would be for the masculine and feminine principles of a person to act in a coordinated and harmonious manner. However, unfortunately, the masculine principle of the average person is too inert and lazy to act, and their display of volitional power is weak. As a result, most are directed by the minds and wills of others, allowing them to think and will in their stead. How many original thoughts or actions does the average person produce? Are not the majority of men simply a shadow or echo of those who possess a stronger mind or will than their own? The disturbance arises from the fact that the average person relies almost exclusively on their consciousness of the "me" and does not understand that they actually possess an "I". They are polarized in their mental feminine principle, while their masculine principle, where the will resides, remains inactive and passive.

The powerful man in the world always manifests the masculine principle of will, and his strength largely depends on this fact. Instead of living under the influences of other minds, he dominates his own mind through his will, thus obtaining the mental images he desires and also controlling the minds of others in the same way.

Let's observe a strong man and see how he manages to implant his mental seeds in the minds of the masses, thus forcing them to think according to his desires. This is the reason why the masses are like flocks of sheep, never generating their own ideas nor using their own powers and mental activities.

The manifestation of mental gender can be observed daily everywhere. Magnetic people are those who can use their masculine principle to impress their ideas upon others. The actor who makes the audience laugh or cry is utilizing this principle. The same is true for the speaker, politician, preacher, or any other person who captures public attention. The peculiar influence one man has over another is due to the manifestation of mental gender along the previously mentioned vibrational lines. In this principle lies the secret of personal magnetism, fascination, etc., as well as the phenomena grouped under the name of hypnotism.

The student who has become acquainted with the phenomena commonly called psychic will have discovered the significant role played by the force known as "suggestion" in such phenomena. Suggestion refers to the process or method by which an idea is transferred or imprinted into the mind of another, thus causing that second mind to act in accordance. To intelligently understand the various psychic phenomena arising from suggestion, it is necessary to have a true understanding of this process. However, it is even more crucial to comprehend vibration and mental gender, as the whole principle of suggestion relies on them.

Scholars of suggestion assert that the objective or voluntary mind is the one that exerts mental impression, or suggestion, upon the subjective or involuntary mind. However, they do not describe the process nor offer analogies to facilitate its understanding. If we examine this subject in the light of Hermetic teachings, we will see that the activation of the feminine principle by the vibratory energy of the masculine is in accordance with the universal laws of nature, and the natural world provides us with countless analogies that help us understand this principle.

Indeed, the Hermetic doctrine maintains that the very creation of the universe is governed by this law, and in all creative manifestations on the spiritual, mental, and physical planes, the principle of gender is always present: the expression of masculine and feminine principles. "As above, so below; as below, so above". And even more than that: by understanding this principle, we are able to immediately and intelligently classify various psychological phenomena, rather than feeling confused by them. This principle really works in practice because it is based on the universal and immutable laws of life.

We will not delve now into a detailed elucidation of the various phenomena related to mental influence or psychic activity. There are many books, most of them very good, which have been written recently on the subject. The main facts set out in these works are correct, although the different authors try to explain them according to their own theories. The student can familiarize themselves with these topics and, using the doctrine of mental gender, can conveniently coordinate the chaotic mass of conflicting theories and teachings, and also, can delve completely into the subject if they wish.

The purpose of this work is not to provide an extensive explanation of psychic phenomena, but rather to point out in a simple manner the master key that opens the numerous doors leading to the Temple of Knowledge, should one wish to explore its interior. We believe that by examining the teachings contained in The Kybalion, it is easy to find the explanation for many difficulties that generate confusion. There is no point in going into details about the multiple characteristics of psychic and mental phenomena if the means to understand the topic that attracts the student's attention are provided. With the help of The Kybalion, one can delve into any library, as the ancient light of Egypt will illuminate the confusing pages and dark problems. That is the true purpose of this work. We do not come to expound a new philosophy, but to provide the basic foundations of the ancient universal teaching that clarifies all doctrines and will serve to reconcile all theories, no matter how different or opposed they may seem.

HGYTET
SSMAIRR
EGABIL
GINIBEA

CHAPTER XV

HERMETIC AXIOMS

"The possession of knowledge, unless accompanied by a manifestation and expression in action, is like the hoarding of precious metals: something vain and absurd. Knowledge, like wealth, is intended to be used. The Law of Use is Universal, and one who violates it suffers as a result of their conflict with natural forces".

The Kybalion

The Hermetic Teachings, although always securely kept in the minds of the fortunate possessors, for the reasons we have already explained, were never meant to be merely kept and hidden. The Law of Use is emphasized in the Teachings, as you can see in the earlier quote from The Kybalion, where it is expressed emphatically. Knowledge without Use and Expression is something vain, providing no benefit to either the possessor or humanity. Beware of mental greed, and put into action what you have learned. Study the Axioms and Aphorisms, but also practice them.

Here are some of the most important Hermetic Axioms, taken from The Kybalion, with some added commentary to each one. Make them your own, practice them, and use them, as they will not truly be yours until you have employed them.

"To change your mood or mental state, change your vibration".
The Kybalion.

One can change their mental vibrations through an act of will, deliberately directing their attention to a more desirable state. Will directs attention, and attention changes vibration. Cultivate the art of attention through will, and you will have discovered the secret to mastering moods and mental states.

"To eliminate an unwanted vibration, apply the principle of polarity and direct your attention toward the opposite pole from what you wish to suppress. The undesirable fades away by changing its polarity".

This is one of the most important Hermetic formulas, based on true scientific principles. As mentioned earlier, a mental state and its opposite are simply two poles of the same thing, and through mental transmutation, that polarity can be reversed. Modern psychologists understand this principle and apply it to eliminate undesirable habits, advising their disciples to focus on the opposite quality. If someone is afraid, it's useless to waste time trying to eliminate fear; instead, they should cultivate courage, and then fear will disappear. Some authors have illustrated this idea with the example of a dark room. It's not worth trying to expel the darkness; it's much better to open the windows and let in the light, and darkness will vanish on its own. To remove a negative quality, one must concentrate on the positive pole of that same quality, and the vibrations will gradually change from negative to positive until they finally polarize at the positive pole instead of the negative one. The reverse is also true, as many have experienced pain by constantly vibrating at the negative pole of things. By changing polarity, one can control mental attitudes and states, completely reshaping one's personal disposition and thus building character. Much of the mastery that advanced Hermetics have over their mentality is due to the intelligent application of polarity, which is one of the most important aspects of mental transmutation. Remember the Hermetic axiom quoted above, which says:

> "The mind, like metals and elements, can be transformed from degree to degree, from condition to condition, from pole to pole, from vibration to vibration".

Mastering polarity involves mastering the principles of mental transmutation or mental alchemy, because without acquiring the art of changing our own polarity, we cannot influence the environment around us. If we understand this principle, we can alter our polarity and that of others, provided we dedicate the time, care, study, and practice necessary to master this art. The principle is true, but the results we achieve depend on the student's patience and constant perseverance.

> "Rhythm can be neutralized through the application of the Art of Polarization".
>
> *The Kybalion.*

As we have explained in the previous chapters, the Hermeticists maintain that the principle of Rhythm manifests itself both on the Mental Plane and on the Physical Plane, and that the linked succession of moods, feelings, emotions, and other mental states is the product of the swinging motion of the mental pendulum, which carries us from one extreme to another. The Hermeticists also teach that the law of neutralization gives us the ability to largely overcome the influence of Rhythm on our consciousness. As we have explained before, there is a higher plane of consciousness and a lower one, and the master, mentally rising to the higher plane, allows the oscillation of the mental pendulum to manifest on the lower plane while he remains on the higher, thus freeing his consciousness from the contrary swing.

This is achieved by polarizing oneself in the Higher Self, thus raising the mental vibrations of the Ego above the plane of ordinary consciousness. It's like rising above something and allowing it to pass beneath. The advanced Hermeticist polarizes in the positive pole of their being, in the I AM, rather than in the pole of their personality, and by denying and rejecting the influence of Rhythm, they rise above their plane of consciousness, standing firm in their assertion of being, while the oscillation occurs on the lower plane without changing their own polarity. This is accomplished by all individuals who have attained a certain degree of self-mastery, whether they understand the law or not. They simply refuse to be carried away by the oscillation and, firmly asserting their superiority, remain polarized in the positive. The master, of course, achieves a higher degree of perfection because they fully understand the law they are mastering with the help of a Higher Law, and through their will, they achieve a balance and firmness that are almost unimaginable to those who are tossed back and forth by emotional oscillations.

Always remember that the Principle of Rhythm cannot be destroyed, as it is indestructible. It can only be overcome by balancing it with another law, thus maintaining equilibrium. The laws of balance operate in both the mental and physical planes, and understanding these laws allows one to transcend them, counteracting their effects.

> "Nothing escapes the Principle of Cause and Effect, but there are many Planes of Causation, and one can use the laws of the higher planes to overcome the laws of the lower ones".
>
> *The Kybalion*

Understanding the practice of polarization, the hermeticist rises to the higher plane of causality, thereby balancing the laws of the lower planes. By elevating above the plane of common causes, one becomes, to a certain extent, a cause rather than merely an effect. By mastering their own emotions and mental states, and neutralizing rhythm, one can largely avoid the operations of the law of cause and effect on the ordinary plane. The masses are swept along, obeying the environment around them, the wills and desires of those who are stronger, the influences of inherited tendencies, or the suggestions and other external causes. They are merely pawns in the game of life. In contrast, advanced hermeticists seek a higher plane of mental action, rising above these causes and mastering their own qualities. In this way, they create new character, qualities, and powers with which they rise above their ordinary environment, becoming directors rather than being directed. These individuals consciously participate in the game of life instead of being carried along by influences, powers, or external wills. They utilize the principle of cause and effect rather than being dominated by it. Of course, even the highest beings are subject to this principle on the higher planes, but on the lower planes, they are lords and not slaves. As The Kybalion says:

> "The wise serve on the higher planes, but rule on the lower ones. They obey the laws that come from above, but on their own plane and over those below them, they rule and give orders. And yet, in doing so, they form part of the Principle instead of opposing it. The wise man adjusts to the Law, and understanding its movements, he executes it instead of being its blind slave. Just as the skilled swimmer moves in different directions, going and coming at will, rather than being like a log that is carried here and there, so is the wise man compared to the common man. And yet, both the swimmer and the log, the wise man and the fool, are subject to the Law. He who understands this is well on the way to Mastery".
>
> *The Kybalion.*

In conclusion, once again, we draw your attention to the Hermetic Axiom:

"True Hermetic Transmutation is a Mental Art".
The Kybalion.

In the aforementioned axiom, the hermetists teach that the great work of influencing the environment is achieved through Mental Power. Being the Universe entirely mental, it follows that it can only be governed by Mentality. And in this truth lies an explanation for all the phenomena and manifestations of the various mental powers that are attracting so much attention and study in these early years of the 20th century. Behind and beneath the teachings of the various cults and schools, the Principle of the Mental Substance of the Universe always remains constant. If the Universe is Mental in its substantial nature, then it follows that Mental Transmutation must change the conditions and phenomena of the Universe. If the Universe is Mental, then the Mind must be the highest force affecting its phenomena. If this is understood, then all so called "miracles" and "amazing feats" are clearly seen for what they are

"THE ALL is MIND; the UNIVERSE is MENTAL".

End of The Kybalion

CONNECTIONS AND SYNERGIES

In the folds of time and eternity, ancient treasures of wisdom intertwine; these age-old texts stand as luminous beacons, guiding those thirsty for knowledge in a sea of questions and enigmas. Their fusion, a delicate web of connections and synergies, awakens curiosity and ignites the spark of learning in minds eager to discover the mysteries of the universe.

At the threshold of this journey, we encounter Hermetic philosophy as the common foundation of the works addressed in this book. This compass guides us in the quest for ultimate truth, inviting us to lift the veils that conceal the secrets of the cosmos. Under its guidance, we delve into the principle of mentalism, that astonishing revelation that whispers to us: "everything is mind". Our reality becomes a canvas shaped by our thoughts and perceptions, and in each stroke lies the power to create our own existence.

Advancing along the path of knowledge, we encounter the law of correspondence, an invisible thread weaving subtle connections between different planes of existence. Understanding this law allows us to discover that what happens in the outer world finds its echo in the realms of the mental and spiritual, and vice versa. In our hands rests the key that opens the door to synchrony, exposing the hidden links between different aspects of our reality. On every page, the call to inner transformation emerges, an invitation to delve deep into our being. We venture into the abyss of our own consciousness, exploring the labyrinths of thoughts, emotions, and perceptions. These tools of self-discovery and growth lead us on the path of wisdom and illumination.

Like the two sides of a coin, the texts unveil to us the dual nature of the universe. We embark on a journey of complementary polarities, where good is linked with evil, light is connected with darkness, and the masculine converses with the feminine. We understand that it is in the harmony of these opposites where we find the true essence of life and attain the desired balance.

In the stillness of meditation and contemplation, we find refuge to explore the depths of our mind and spirit. We immerse ourselves in the profound silence, observing our thoughts like leaves floating on the river of consciousness. It is in these moments of serenity that we draw closer to our purest essence, to the connection with the divine that resides within us.

The laws of cause and effect, like invisible threads that bind our existence, remind us that every choice, every thought, and action resonates in the universe. We are architects of our own reality and bear the responsibility for our deeds. Awareness of this law invites us to forge a conscious future, where our actions transcend the limits of our being and embrace the entirety of the cosmos. In the symphony of the universe, we discover the unity and connection that links us to all that exists. We are intertwined threads in the grand cosmic fabric, and every movement, every thought, every beat of our heart weaves the melody of existence. We become vibrating instruments in this universal orchestra, where our essence intertwines with that of the whole.

The law of vibration invites us to understand that everything in the universe is in constant motion, in perpetual flow of energy. From the tiniest atoms to distant galaxies, every particle dances to the cosmic rhythm of vibration. It urges us to tune into our own frequencies, to find harmony within ourselves, and to resonate in accordance with the universe that surrounds us.

In the ebb and flow of life, we encounter the law of polarity, which teaches us that everything has its opposite, and these opposites are two sides of the same coin. We recognize that duality is inherent in existence and that, in the balance of these opposing forces, our own evolution is forged. In the quest for transcendence, we learn to embrace the extremes, to find harmony at the intersection of light and shadow.

The law of rhythm immerses us in the understanding of the natural cycles that govern our reality. We discover that everything flows in a constant ebb and flow, in a rhythmic sway that sets the beats of our existence. We adapt to these rhythms, dancing gracefully in the tides of time, recognizing that changes and transformations are an intrinsic part of our journey.

Alchemical transmutation is revealed as the supreme art of inner transformation. We immerse ourselves in the crucible of self-awareness, purifying our emotions and thoughts, distilling the essence of our being. In this alchemical process, we become alchemists of our own lives, seeking spiritual elevation and communion with the divine. On this journey toward wisdom, the quest for truth becomes our guiding light. We venture into the labyrinths of knowledge, challenging established certainties, exploring different perspectives, and exposing the hidden secrets of existence. We become tireless seekers, eternal apprentices of the vast cosmos that surrounds us.

In the vastness of this ocean of wisdom, the courageous reader enthusiastically plunges. It is not a journey of mere information accumulation but a quest for understanding, for a deep connection with the very essence of the universe. Thus, with prose that caresses the senses and narration that ignites the imagination, these sacred texts come to life in the minds and hearts of those who dare to venture into their pages. They are not just words in ink on paper but master keys that unlock the doors of ancient knowledge and invite us to explore the boundaries of our existence.

Intuition rises as our most faithful ally on this path of discovery. It whispers transcendental truths in our ear, guiding us along less traveled roads. We learn to trust our inner voice, that divine spark that connects us to the primordial source of knowledge. It is through intuition that we unveil the deepest secrets and access a knowledge that goes beyond words and rational explanations.

PRACTICES

Hermetic and alchemical principles are not just abstract concepts; they have practical applications in our daily lives. Here are some ways in which we can apply these principles to find greater balance and well-being in our lives:

1. Reflection on the principle of mentalism: "Imagine for a moment that your thoughts are seeds planted in the garden of your mind. If you sow seeds of joy and gratitude, you will harvest a reality full of positivity and well-being. But if you allow seeds of negativity and pessimism to grow, you will find yourself surrounded by constant obstacles and challenges. Remember that you are the gardener of your mind, and your thoughts are the seeds you choose to plant".
2. Reflection on the law of correspondence: "Contemplate the reflection of the moon on a tranquil lake. Observe how every movement and glimmer on the water's surface has its counterpart in the moon's radiance in the sky. Just as the lake reflects the moonlight, our actions and emotions are reflected in the subtle planes of existence. Let us remember that we are part of an interconnected whole, and every choice we make reverberates through the invisible threads of the universe".
3. Reflection on inner transformation: "Imagine you are a caterpillar enclosed in its cocoon, feeling the call to transform into a beautiful butterfly. Within you, there is a latent power, a force that drives you to break through the barriers that limit you. As you shed your old self and your old beliefs, you undergo an internal metamorphosis. In the end, you emerge as a butterfly, ready to fly to new horizons and spread your wings in freedom. Such is inner transformation, a journey toward our true essence".

4. The importance of self-awareness: These works invite us to be aware of our thoughts, emotions, and actions. They remind us that we are the architects of our reality and that our choices have an impact on our life and the world around us. Self-awareness allows us to take control of our destiny and steer ourselves toward wisdom and fulfillment.

5. The pursuit of inner harmony: Exploring the universal laws leads us to recognize the importance of finding balance in all areas of our life. Harmony between opposites, acknowledging our internal dualities, and integrating all our facets lead us to greater peace and personal fulfillment.

6. The connection between the individual and the universe: The texts reveal the profound interconnection that exists between us and the cosmos. They invite us to recognize our unity with the whole, to understand that our actions and thoughts resonate in the universe, and to live in harmony with natural rhythms and cycles. This connection opens us to a broader perspective and provides us with a deeper understanding of our purpose in existence.

7. The power of personal transformation: Through introspection, meditation, and the practice of Hermetic teachings, we can experience profound inner transformation. Alchemical transmutation serves as a powerful metaphor for this process. Just as the alchemist seeks to turn lead into gold, we seek to transmute our limitations into virtues, our weaknesses into strengths, and our shadows into light. This personal transformation opens us up to new possibilities and allows us to achieve a higher level of consciousness and fulfillment.

8. The importance of intuition and connection with the divine: Reading these passages reminds us that beyond rationality and intellect, there is a powerful resource within us: intuition.

They invite us to trust that inner voice that guides us towards truth and connects us with universal wisdom. By tuning into our intuition, we open ourselves to a deeper connection with the divine, with the cosmos, and with our own essential being.

9. The unceasing quest for truth and knowledge: These teachings call upon us to be eternal seekers of truth. They invite us to question established beliefs, explore new paths, and expand our understanding of the world and ourselves. The pursuit of knowledge takes us on a journey of constant learning and allows us to uncover the hidden mysteries of existence.
10. The importance of balance and integration: In the backdrop of these texts, we find a constant invitation to balance and integration. They remind us that it is in the union of opposites, in the recognition and harmonization of our internal dualities, where we find wholeness and wisdom. The integration of masculine and feminine aspects, of light and shadow, allows us to live a balanced and authentic life.

PRACTICAL APPLICATIONS

1. Recognize the power of your thoughts and words. Cultivate a positive and conscious mindset, focusing on thoughts and affirmations that strengthen and propel you towards success. Practice creative visualization, imagining and drawing your goals and desires toward you.

2. . Reflect on how your thoughts, emotions, and actions are reflected in your environment and in your relationships. If you wish to experience harmony and love in your life, cultivate those same feelings and attitudes towards others. Understand that what you give, you receive.

3. Inner transformation: Take time for introspection and self-awareness. Observe your patterns of thought and behavior, and seek areas in which you wish to grow and improve. Practice meditation and mindfulness to calm the mind and connect with your innermost authentic self.

4. Dual nature: Accept and embrace both your aspects of light and your shadows. Recognize that we all have strengths and weaknesses, and that both are an integral part of our humanity. Work on the balance between both aspects, cultivating your virtues and facing your challenges with compassion and humility.

5. Be aware of the choices you make and the actions you take in your life. Recognize that each of them has consequences, both for yourself and for others. Cultivate personal responsibility and make decisions that align with your values and ethical principles.

6. Unity and Connection: Practice empathy and compassion towards others, recognizing that we are all interconnected in this vast fabric of existence. Cultivate healthy and nurturing relationships and seek opportunities to collaborate and contribute to the collective well-being.

7. Alchemical Transmutation: Work on the transformation of your negative or limiting aspects. Identify the patterns and beliefs that hold you back and seek ways to change them. Alchemize the lead of negativity into the gold of positivity, personal growth, and self-improvement.

MEDITATIONS AND REFLECTIONS

1. Exercise in Thought Observation: Dedicate a few minutes each day to sit in silence and observe your thoughts without judgment. Allow them to pass like clouds in the sky, without clinging to any in particular. Observe how positive and negative thoughts arise and fade away. This practice will help you develop awareness of your mental patterns and cultivate a calmer and more balanced mind

2. Energy Connection Meditation: Sit in a quiet place and close your eyes. Take deep breaths and feel the energy flowing through your body with each inhale and exhale. Visualize your energy expanding beyond your body, connecting you to the energy of the universe. Feel that deep connection and recognize that you are part of something much greater.

3. Reflection on duality: Take a moment to reflect on your aspects of light and shadow. Make a list of your strengths and virtues, as well as your weaknesses and challenges. Acknowledge that both aspects are a part of you, and that each has its purpose in your growth and evolution. Ask yourself how you can use your strengths to face your challenges and how you can embrace your weaknesses as opportunities for growth.

4. Gratitude and high-vibration exercise: Each day, take a moment to write down three things you are grateful for. They can be simple things, like a moment of happiness, a meaningful encounter, or an everyday blessing. As you write, feel the gratitude in your heart and let that emotion raise your vibration. This exercise will help you cultivate a positive mindset and attract more positive experiences into your life.

5. Inner balance meditation: Sit in a comfortable posture and bring your attention to your breath. Visualize a balance between your body, mind, and spirit. Imagine how these aspects

of yourself come together in harmony, creating a sense of peace and well-being. Allow yourself to feel the connection and unity within you, recognizing that each aspect is essential in your existence.

6. Reflection on interconnectedness: Reflect on the relationships in your life and how you connect with others. Consider how your words and actions can impact those around you. Contemplate how you can cultivate more authentic and meaningful relationships, based on compassion, empathy, and mutual support. Recognize that we are interconnected beings, and our actions can generate a positive effect in the world.

7. Transmutation exercise: Identify a limiting belief or negative pattern in your life and write it down on a piece of paper. Then, visualize how that belief or pattern transforms into a positive and empowered version. Imagine yourself breaking free from that limiting belief and adopting a new, more empowering and positive mindset. Picture how this transformation allows you to grow, expand, and live life to the fullest. Write down the new positive belief or affirmation you wish to cultivate on another piece of paper and place it in a visible spot as a daily reminder of your transmutation process.

8. Intuition connection meditation: Sit in silence, close your eyes, and direct your attention inward. Take deep breaths and relax your body and mind. Visualize a bright light at your heart center, representing your inner intuition and wisdom. Ask your intuition to guide you and provide clarity in any situation you need. Listen carefully to any messages or sensations that arise. Trust your intuition as a reliable guide on your journey.

9. Reflection on purpose and the search for truth: Take time to reflect on your purpose in life and what truly impassions you. Make a list of activities, interests, and values that make you feel alive and connected to a higher purpose. Ask yourself how

you can live in alignment with those values and how you can seek truth and knowledge in your daily life.

10. Balance and Self-Management Exercise: Make a list of different areas of your life, such as work, family, health, relationships, and personal time. Evaluate how you're doing in each of these areas and what actions you can take to balance and manage them more effectively. Identify the areas where you need to allocate more time and attention, and set clear goals to achieve that balance.

"Together we are more powerful, sharing our energy we empower humanity. We are part of an infinite universal network that needs us and in turn, we are nourished by it".

"When the energy of the life force is 'off-center,' the task becomes an effort".

"Culture constructs our own judgments and prejudices, forgetting who we truly are. The only truth lies within us".

"The Infinite Energy is always present, waiting to be used, but it acts in an individual's life only under their Conscious Command".

Made in the USA
Monee, IL
19 February 2024

53747426R00105